HOW NOT TO BE
AFRAID *of*
YOUR OWN LIFE

HOW NOT TO BE AFRAID *of* YOUR OWN LIFE

Opening Your Heart to Confidence, Intimacy, and Joy

SUSAN PIVER

ST. MARTIN'S PRESS

New York

"Meeting Relationships with Loving Kindness," in Chapter 5, appeared in slightly different form in the *Shambhala Sun* magazine in February 2006.

ISBN-13: 978-0-312-35596-8

TO

SAKYONG MIPHAM RINPOCHE,

who opened the gate to the treasury of oral instructions,

TO MY PARENTS,

LOUISE AND JULIUS PIVER,

for their unceasing generosity,

AND TO

DUNCAN BROWNE,

who knows how to love

CONTENTS

Grant your blessing so that my mind may be one with the dharma.
Grant your blessing so that dharma may progress along the path.
Grant your blessing so that the path may clarify confusion.
Grant your blessing so that confusion may dawn as wisdom.

—THE FOUR DHARMAS OF GAMPOPA

Introduction

EACH OF US IS born seeking a meaningful life. We have a natural ability to sense what is significant, live in peace, and surround ourselves with love. We come into this world wanting these things and only these things. No baby (that I know of) ever wished for a cooler car seat, hated her thighs, or doubted a mother's love. From the moment we arrive, we are instinctively drawn toward warmth, closeness, and acceptance. When the world doesn't provide what we seek, we're shocked. The rejection is completely unexpected, and we withdraw. Once we have met with a negative reception, our initial response to new faces and first-time experiences becomes fear, not love. At this point we have lost touch with reality, not the other way around, because to live in fear is to live in a delusional state. When we are fearful, we simply can't see who or what is in front of us—all we see is our fear, and that is what we react to, plan for, and anticipate.

Fear can be conquered. We can meet any situation, important or trivial, old or new, surprising or predictable, with self-confidence, gentleness, and elegance. And we don't have to change one thing about ourselves to do so. In fact, we already possess all the courage we'll ever need, and it—not fear—can animate the way we think about ourselves, others, and the world. The ancient practice of meditation can show us how.

Meditation will be our working basis, the foundation for this exploration. Instead of constantly evaluating yourself for inherent worth or worthlessness, meditation helps to plant self-view in equanimity. Instead of creating a new and better you, meditation reveals your innate perfection. Perhaps most important, instead of reacting to others with impatience, judgment, anger, or desperation, meditation teaches you to blossom open to whomever you encounter and transform the energies you meet into patience, power, and kindness.

Remember, we were born without fear and have a natural ability to love. Returning to our inborn fearless state requires unlearning certain things, not acquiring new skills. We don't have to become daring where we're risk-averse, calm when we're anxious, or self-loving if we have self-doubt. Instead, we can relax. We can learn how to be who we already are, honestly, unapologetically, and intelligently, embracing everything that's wonderful about our life and everything that's a mess. We can stop defending the personal or professional territory we own or wish to own. We don't have to feel afraid of change, loss, rejection, or stress. Nor do we have to fear what may happen to us in the course of daily life; we can cultivate a kind of intelligence and skill that neutralizes fear on the spot.

Aggression, self-righteousness, and pride are not signs of fearlessness. Gentleness, joy, and self-confidence are. These qualities arise from the genuine effort to make friends with ourselves and to accept ourselves exactly as we are, right at this moment. This is the key to fearlessness and this is the skill taught by meditation.

It's All Personal

I have spent ten years practicing Buddhist meditation and studying the philosophy behind it. While it may seem unlikely that a twenty-five-hundred-year-old tradition could have anything to do with the stresses of twenty-first-century life, with the fear of terrorism, insane credit card debts, and endless e-mail, I found that the practices associated with this deep, compelling, and nondogmatic tradition began to soften my worst fears and longest-standing neuroses. I learned how to address directly what frightens me with generosity and patience. It's not that being afraid now feels good, but I am confident I have what I need to meet my fears wholeheartedly and transform them. I'd like to share with you what I've been taught, offer my understanding of some traditional Buddhist teachings in plain language, and show you what has helped me to stop being afraid of my own life.

When I began to read about Buddhism in the early nineties, I was surprised by what I found—not by the content but by how human, modern, and relevant it was. I expected to read an exotic fairy tale or myth, one that might leave me inspired but unclear about how to apply these long-ago and faraway stories to my relationships or work life.

However, what I read wasn't foreign at all. In a first-millennium, Hindu prince kind of way, the Buddha essentially asked the same questions about his life that I was asking about mine. What is the meaning and purpose of my life? Who am I? How can I find happiness? Instead of gazing up at a mystery, I found myself eye to eye with a fellow traveler. If the Buddha could do it, perhaps I could too. In any case, I reasoned, even if I didn't attain full enlightenment, as the Buddha had, I could probably become less stressed out.

And it's important to note that in Buddhist philosophy and practice there is no external being to believe in and no heaven to try to get into. Before meditation practice can begin, no doctrine needs to be accepted. In fact, doctrines, it's said, are a hindrance. One can continue to be Jewish, Baptist, Muslim, or atheist; the Buddhist teachings don't replace or contradict any particular school of thought. The Buddha isn't thought of as a divine being who will answer our prayers if we follow his teachings—he's an inspiring example of someone who worked through every single layer of his neuroses and discovered lasting peace of mind. If he could do it, we can too.

The Buddha's Path

The Prince Siddhartha Gautama (another name for the Buddha) lived a very sheltered life. He was served the best food, clothed in the finest fabrics, and surrounded by dancing girls. Members of the court were forbidden to tell him bad news or mention any type of problem in his presence. Siddhartha was shielded from all things ugly or painful. He had never seen a sick person.

One day he was being driven to a garden where he liked to spend time. On the way, he saw some people carrying an old man who was quite ill and dying. The prince had never seen anything like this, and he asked his charioteer, Chandaka, what was wrong with this man. Chandaka explained that he was old, near death. The Buddha was shocked. "How did he get this way?" he asked. Chandaka replied that we all age and die. When Siddhartha heard this, he was stunned. Everyone? How could this be? There must be something more than this! On the spot, he vowed to determine how to transcend the cycle of life and death, and show others how to do it too. He didn't vacillate or waste time. That very night, he discarded his princely robes, jewels, and privileges, and left home. He set out on his path.

Over a period of years, Siddhartha tried and mastered numerous yogic and ascetic disciplines, always attempting to see what lies beyond this cycle. Although he reached deeper and deeper levels of understanding and realization, he still couldn't quite figure out how to put an end to suffering. Finally, he decided to sit down under a particular tree and not move until he reached ultimate clarity. So he sat. He sat for many days. The Buddha's mind relaxed more and more deeply. It became perfectly clear and calm. On the night of a full moon in May, he realized that he was actually approaching enlightenment, complete freedom from suffering.

At that very moment, the Maras, beings who represent obstacles and difficulties, arose to put a stop to his enlightenment. They caused storms to rage and sent monstrous ghouls to frighten him. The Buddha did not move. They tried to shoot him with arrows, but in midair the arrows turned to flowers that simply fell to the ground at his feet. The Maras began taunting the Buddha. They told him he was presumptuous to think he could attain such a lofty state. They tried to make him believe that he was inept, going down the wrong path, a fool for working so hard, and that he was making a big deal about things that weren't important. Finally, the Maras tried to intimidate the Buddha by telling him that he was not entitled to the ground on which he sat, and in fact he had no right to be there at all. But although they tried to scare the Buddha off through physical threats, uncomfortable conditions, intimidation, hysteria, and confusion, he remained focused and peaceful, completely intent on learning the secret to calm all suffering. He became enlightened.

The things the Maras said to the Buddha are the things we say to ourselves all day long. The traps they laid out for the Buddha are the traps we lay out for ourselves. We let ourselves be scared, mostly because we judge, criticize, and lose patience with our own thoughts. Instead of turning into flowers, the arrows of fear, doubt, and hesitation pierce us over and over again. But we can do what the Buddha did. Through meditation, we can learn to watch our thoughts as they arise and catch them before they overwhelm us. Like the Buddha, we can stop, turn around, take a seat, and look our situation right in the eye.

The Gift of Meditation

How can meditation—which may look like sitting around doing nothing—lead to all these wonderful things? It does so because as it quiets the mind, your deep wisdom and unchanging basic goodness are naturally revealed. We experience our own goodness all the time, but usually these moments are so ordinary and simple that we miss them completely. When you walk outside and smile at the sudden hit of sunshine, when you hear music so pure it makes you cry, or when you experience the joy of being kissed back, you are connecting with this goodness. Usually these moments come as sudden surprises, but a mind calmed by meditation can find them in every experience. Meditation teaches you how to stop listening to your to-do lists, parental warnings, or past wounds for guidance. You can listen to what is fresh, what is wise. You can listen to yourself.

What I've learned from my teachers is that meditation is actually the boldest, most straightforward way to face yourself squarely. It is the way to know the self that resides just below the surface, a surface that is usually choppy with likes and dislikes, hopes and fears, and judgments of all sorts. This amalgam of thought and emotion is who we think we are, but we are wrong. Who we are is far more interesting, exciting, and powerful than this. Who we are is fearless, joyful, and extremely kind.

Searching for a Spiritual Path

When I examine my life, I see that it has been a story about interacting with fear, fighting with it, being overwhelmed, defeated, and outraged by it. Fear has come in predictable forms, such as childhood nightmares and desperate shyness, or in sudden, shocking ways, such as traumatized reactions and startling phobias. It has washed over me in waves, pierced my heart like an icy dagger, and choked my breathing. I've gone through periods of intense fear about my lovability, employability, intelligence, financial security, even my weight. Fear has dared and tested me, and confronting it has altered the arc and scope of my existence into something more expansive and satisfying than I ever expected. It has certainly propelled me onto the spiritual path and indeed has revealed itself as my most profound and uncompromising teacher.

I was an exceptionally fearful child, depressed, confused, and very shy. I was an utter failure at school, a total flop. My grades rarely rose above Cs and Ds, and I actually flunked eighth grade. I failed at the everyday activities that others seemed to have no trouble succeeding at, such as taking tests, making friends, and having fun. I learned to hide my real interests— reading and writing—and simply keep quiet. My favorite place to hang out was on the floor under my desk, an L-shaped built-in, flush against the wall, with drawers all the way to the floor on both sides. I would pull out the chair, curl up with a favorite book in the space underneath, and pull the chair in again so no one could see me.

Hiding became something I did well for many years. As I got older, instead of taking cover under furniture, I hid behind various lifestyles, beliefs, and viewpoints. My fear has resulted in foolish career choices, unhappy relationships, and unexplored opportunities. I've tried to escape my fears in different ways, hoping to banish them by becoming a born-again Christian, a Guardian Angel (member of a voluntary street patrol), a music-business executive, and a self-help author. I looked everywhere for the right path to a joyous and peaceful life.

My first step along the spiritual path began with a collision. I was twenty-six years old, working as a cocktail waitress at a nightclub in Austin, Texas, when driving home from work at 3:00 A.M., I was in an accident, hit broadside by a drunk driver. What happened at the moment of impact and beyond I know only from what I read in police reports and hospital records. I don't remember any of it: getting into the ambulance or being rushed into surgery, my boyfriend arriving at the hospital, or the looks on my parents' faces when they were advised to prepare for my death. I sustained a liver laceration, fractured pelvis, broken ribs, and more. I was in surgery three times in twenty-four hours in an effort to stop internal bleeding. Friends and family were told to disregard visiting-hour rules: if they wanted to see me, they'd better get in quick.

I was lucky, though. I didn't die, and several months later, after more scary operations, I was discharged, physically scarred and mentally in shock but relatively intact. My boyfriend drove me home and as he helped me settle on the couch in our living room, we began to notice something unusual. The room seemed to be glowing and the light was getting rosier and rosier, sweeter and sweeter, until we felt giddy. Gradually it illuminated everything we could see. We were doing perfectly ordinary things: sitting on the couch, having a drink of water, petting the cats. Except everything was extraordinarily vibrant, and somehow this vibrancy felt blissful. It may sound crazy, but we both experienced it. I asked him, "Are we in some kind of ecstasy or something?" He said he thought we were. Neither of us wanted to go to sleep. But eventually we couldn't help it, and when we woke up it was gone. He's not my boyfriend anymore, but even now, nearly twenty years later, when we talk we sometimes remind each other of that time when ordinary was perfection, perfection was ordinary, and we felt the presence of something that could most closely be called spirit. I believe that in those moments my soul reentered my body and my life force was returned to me, stronger and clearer than before. Up until this time, I would have scoffed at such a report as hopelessly New Agey and silly, but now this is the only way I can think of to describe it.

These two events—the car accident and the glimpse of bliss—each shifted my awareness. Even now I feel that, in some way, my life restarted when I came home from the hospital. After having been close to death, I believe I reentered my life through some sort of ecstasy. From this point forward, I began to feel led by something greater than myself.

Discovering a Path

A few years after these experiences, I was sitting at a dining table at the Kripalu Center for Yoga & Health in western Massachusetts. I had visited Kripalu several times before to learn yoga; my brother suggested that it would be helpful in recovery. It was 1986, before the yoga craze—so I wasn't quite sure whether he was suggesting I do some stretching or join a cult. I took a chance and fell in love with yoga on the spot. I traveled back to Kripalu to rest, read, and practice yoga as often as I could. One afternoon I was sitting alone in the dining hall, reading a book called *Cutting Through Spiritual Materialism* by Chögyam Trungpa Rinpoche. I had no idea who Chögyam Trungpa Rinpoche was, but the moment I picked the book up, I was struck by the freshness, vividness, and poetry of the author's voice. He discussed interesting but foreign topics such as karma, compassion, and enlightenment. Then I read this:

> *There is a saying in the Tibetan Scriptures: "Knowledge must be burned, hammered, and beaten like pure gold. Then one can wear it as an ornament." So when you receive spiritual instruction . . . you do not take it uncritically, but you burn it, you hammer it, you beat it, until the bright, dignified color of gold appears. . . . Therefore dharma is applicable to every age, to every person; it has a living quality. It is not enough to imitate your master or guru . . . the teachings are an individual experience.*

Of course. One's own mind is the only reliable guide. The place to start is with who you already are and what you are experiencing right now. No doctrine. No ideal to emulate. I had never heard anyone

say that before. On the Buddhist path particular qual-
ifications, beliefs, or vows are not necessary. Strength
and independence of mind are the qualities that are
required. Maybe my inabilities to toe the line, fit in,
succeed in conventional life were not such bad things
after all. They were just me, and on this path, "just
me" is the path. You start with who you are, and the
goal is self-discovery. This made a lot of sense to me.
I guess I'm a Buddhist, I thought to myself, I just never
knew that was what it was called.

The wish to find a spiritual path that could help me
discover my real, authentic life and a fearless way of living was fulfilled when I discovered the Buddhist path—
but you certainly don't need to become a Buddhist to
benefit from its teachings and lessons, to acquire com-
monsense tools for confronting difficult relationships,
taking professional risks, accepting yourself as you are,
or simply sleeping better at night! The practices in this
book explain how to open and connect to the magic of
authenticity and joy. These practices confer wisdom for
navigating everyday life in a way that is flexible and
modern. The Buddhist teachings on how to work with
your own mind are kind, challenging, canny, and vast.
And, as mentioned, they function without asking you to
believe anything in particular; nothing but your own
experience really counts.

Trust but Verify

The very first thing I was taught was to take whatever I learned and check it against my actual experience. If the lesson was useful and true, I was invited to keep it. If not, I was invited with equal friendliness to discard it. It's of vital importance, I learned, not to adopt any view just because it sounds good. I was to verify it against my real-life experience. In that spirit, I invite you to see if the suggestions in this book are helpful for you personally. What is useful, keep. What is not, discard.

This book can be read as you wish—you could read it straight through or start at the end. You could read the whole thing and ignore the seven-day program suggested in Chapter 8. Or you could go straight to the seven-day program and treat the other chapters as backstory. Take your time and test out the notions presented. Does meditation have an effect on your fear levels? Does it enable you to think differently about old problems? Is your self-confidence strengthened in a reliable way?

As you undertake this process, I'll offer you a single warning: a meditation practice can have serious repercussions. If you try the practice a few times and think, Cool, but not for me, that is completely okay. If you want to practice meditation occasionally as a stress-reduction tool, that's also fine. But if you decide you want to make it an ongoing part of your life, think carefully. Examine your motivation and inspiration levels before setting out on the journey. Meditation practice creates a new way of relating to yourself, your relationships, and your work life. Think long and hard about whether or not you really want to examine your own experience this closely. Know that, if you do, the way you see yourself will change, as will the way others see you. It may not happen right away, but in time it will. How much stamina and discipline are you prepared to bring to the table? Most important, how honest are you willing to be with yourself?

An ongoing meditation practice puts you in touch with powerful energies. If you keep up with your practice and your commitment to yourself, these energies can be incredibly supportive. If a practice is approached casually, they may appear to be more like irritations and obstacles. All I can ask you to do is pose the same question to yourself that my teacher presented me with when I told him I wanted to make a formal commitment to this practice: "Are you ready for your life to change completely?"

The practices and insights contained in this book are in no way of my making. They are the instructions of the Buddha as taught to me by my teachers, with boundless generosity. The way I've interpreted them is another thing altogether, and if any of the views herein are dharmically incorrect, it's entirely the result of my lack of correct understanding.

1

What Creates Fear?

ONE MORNING I TURNED on CNN and saw that the terror alert had been elevated to orange. I'm not sure how bad orange is, but I know it's not good. I stopped in my tracks, looked around my kitchen, and saw a stack of untried recipes, pictures from our recent trip to Colorado, and a shopping list written in my husband's hand. Suddenly all these seemed very precious, and for a moment I allowed myself to imagine the magnitude of our loss if a terrorist attacked Boston. Our lives could end. Our house could be destroyed. Our lifestyle and our sense of refuge could be wiped out. It would be unbearable. It could happen! It happens to others every day. I thought about trying to escape by moving to a small town in British Columbia or Tuscany. I wanted to run away. My imagined loss was so excruciating that I knew I would do almost anything to prevent it. But I couldn't tolerate the feeling of horror for more than a few seconds, so I put it all aside and went upstairs to take a shower.

In the post-9/11 world, flashes of fear like this are commonplace—as is the possibility of becoming hysterical, numb, or self-righteous. The need to discover and cultivate fearlessness is at an all-time high. Back in the mid-nineties, it seemed we were scared of overwork, credit card balances, and the prevalence of divorce. We may still worry about these things, but now the mix is much, much more intense. It includes fear of terrorism and global warfare; of the irreversible loss of natural resources, such as breathable air, drinkable water, and plentiful oil; and although it was unthinkable as little as ten years ago, of the displacement of America as the world's unimpeachable superpower and the security that comes with that role. Just when we think life can't become more stressful, a strange new disease is identified or the price of gasoline rises.

Once I worked at a small company that was being sold to avoid going under. Most of us had worked there since the beginning and had done so with respect and, frequently, joy—until our jobs were threatened. Our collegiality fell away, and we all began to fight for territory, flatter the boss, and blame one another for problems. Our office was awash in what appeared to be unresolved parental issues and desperate attempts to secure a strategic position to survive the transition. It is surprising how quickly fear can destabilize and poison good relationships. If the fear of losing a job can turn you into a coward, what can be expected from those who may lose a child to war or be denied permission to practice their faith?

Yet it doesn't take remarkable events to create fear. Fear escalates in times of discomfort, no matter how remarkable or ordinary. When we think we might be in love, we hold our feelings back until circumstances are just right. When we want to pitch our co-workers a new idea, we worry about the consequences, decide against taking a risk, and hope for a better day. If we hear that a friend is ill, we long for things to go back to the way they were. These responses are completely and utterly understandable; we retreat from love, shrink from creativity, and hide from loss. It seems so much easier to hold to the familiar or cling to old beliefs about yourself and the way life is "supposed" to go. The question is: How do we prevent our fear from sucking us deeper into dogmatism, depression, and hatred, or their relatives, superiority, laziness, and numbness? The answer is to find a response that balances our emotions through relating to what scares us, not through turning away from it.

Before we can craft a response, we should explore what we're up against. There are three arenas within which we encounter our own fear: about ourselves; about others; and about life, or the way we approach the world in general.

Fear of Self

The list of reasons to fear yourself may be quite long. Maybe you fear that you're some kind of phony. Perhaps you fear that you can't handle the difficulties and responsibilities of life. Deep down, we all fear that who we are is simply not good enough. If our bosses knew how inadequate we really were, they would fire us. Lovers would break up with us. Our parents or children would reject us. Self-doubt can become so twisted and uncomfortable that we will do almost anything to avoid examining these fears about ourselves. Tension between the real self and self-image causes frustration to build and build.

Fear of Others

Finally, when the frustration level rises beyond a tolerable point, we start to look around for someone to blame for our unpleasant situation or personal discomfort. (My friend Greg says his family's problem-solving methodology involves three steps: 1. Define problem. 2. Assign blame. 3. Problem solved.) You can build a case against others' failings, but no matter how convincing it may be and how many complex initiatives you mount in the name of problem solving, it won't alleviate your pain. However, with the alternative—not blaming anyone or anything—we might be left with no explanation for our predicament, which is the hardest state of all to tolerate. How would we manage our problems if there is no one at fault: no mother or father to impugn for deficient or excessive attention; no personal attributes (laziness, stupidity, bad luck, psychological defects of all kinds) to hold accountable for our woes; no shortcomings in our political or social structures to bear responsibility?

It's easier to feel cranky about how no-account the others in our lives are than to question why we hang out with them in the first place or what our role is in the current difficulty. Colleagues are stupid, boyfriends always leave, and the government stinks. We all know when we're in the presence of someone who takes no responsibility for difficult situations, but we rarely recognize that behavior in ourselves. Fear projected onto others seems to give us a bit of breathing room and some options. Instead of working to acknowledge and synthesize disappointment, anger, frustration, or heartache, we convince ourselves that everything would be fine if everyone else would simply behave. We turn our attention away from our uncomfortable feelings and toward others with the intention to convince people of their mistakes.

Fear of Life

Finally, even if our life is great, our self-esteem is good, and our relationships a delight, we may still find ourselves afraid of life. Surprisingly, happiness itself can be the most fearsome state of all. There is so much to lose. I often tell my husband, "If I had known I was going to love you this much, I never would have married you," and I'm not really joking. Eventually, he and I are going to die and our relationship will be over. Every time I conjure the image of one of us saying good-bye to the other, I just lose it. I can't hold the image in my mind for longer than it takes to type this sentence. It's too painful. But the eventual loss is real, and there's nothing we can do about it. We have no control over the most important aspects of our lives, the people, places, and activities we hold most dear. Because this is so scary, we try to rely on explanations, platitudes, cynicism, or magical incantations instead of facing reality. We swear to be loyal to our mates, our friends, our families—and seek such a commitment in return as a way of avoiding the frightening aspects of relationships: people could leave or betray us and we have no control over either. We believe that if we eat well, exercise, and think the right thoughts, we can control our health and never get sick. Of course we should be careful in the way we treat our bodies and form relationships, but doing these things can't change the difficult reality that we are not in control.

The Three Mistaken Reactions to Fear

Whether it's fear of self, others, or the realities of life, Buddhism refers to three types of fear reactions:

passion, aggression, and ignorance. While we all have employed all three at various times, you may discover that you have a typical default response to situations or people that frighten you. Try to get a feel for how each kind of fear appears in your life, and if one seems more dominant.

PASSION

Passion doesn't necessarily refer to excitement, infatuation, or emotional intensity. This type of passion is related to clinging, grasping, and desperation. This fear is at work when we want something or someone so bad we can't eat, sleep, or even hold in our awareness anything but our desire. Passion is blinding, seductive, and ultimately, impossible to satisfy. It is entirely centered on what you think you need, want, or must have. It's like when you're driven insane by waiting for someone to telephone and every other caller is such an irritation that you can't wait to get rid of them. Passion blinds you to the existence of anyone or anything but your own gnawing need. This is passion as poison, a version of fear that says, If I don't get what I want I might die, and nothing else matters. It's nonnegotiable.

AGGRESSION

Aggression includes the obvious: engaging in head-on confrontations, fighting with words or fists, taking what doesn't belong to you, and allowing hate against yourself or others to develop. But aggression can also include what you don't do, like abandoning difficult relationships instead of resolving them, skipping an appointment you feel uncomfortable about, or continually delaying the day you're going to quit smoking, start exercising, stop drinking, or forgive your mother. Aggression arises when we meet with anything or anyone that is not to our liking and we want to make it *go away*. In the grip of this poison, we fear unseen enemies and see everything as a threat to our security. We blame, resist, lash out, and employ subterfuge as strategies to keep ourselves protected when we feel that our view of how things should go is not taken into account. While we may have well-thought-out reasons for attempting to strong-arm others to get our way, in the end, this type of behavior is an old-fashioned, pain-inducing, self-centered hissy fit.

Aggression refers to those times when you simply lose sight of anyone but yourself in the effort to secure what you think you must have. You want to walk over the backs of others in high heels and it feels gooood.

IGNORANCE

The third expression of fear, ignorance or delusion, is a tricky one. It refers to what you're blind to, willfully or not. We each have our blind spots, of course. Sweet and funny examples of blind spots can be seen on fashion makeover television programs (which I love). The hosts find women who dress terribly and teach them how to become gorgeous. They show the women what to wear to enhance their natural beauty, which is always, always revealed. When the women stop fearing that they're too old, overweight, or boring to be beautiful, they see their real beauty, which was always there. They burst into tears, along with their family and friends (and me). Why couldn't they see it before? Why, until now, had they seen themselves as ugly and dressed accordingly? Ignorance is whatever transpires in the space between the woman and her image. This may seem like a silly example, but it shows how sometimes we're content to sit around in our own messes. It's too hard to change our view of ourselves or the world. We fall asleep instead of paying attention to problems, "forget" appointments or engagements we'd rather not have made, hide behind low self-esteem, or repeat the same mistake over and over without seeming to learn from it.

The most difficult form of ignorance (and, therefore, of fear) is not even knowing that you *are* afraid. The same difficult situations repeat themselves in your life, and you are unaware that this is because of the choices you make about how to react, behave, and believe. This is a very thorny problem to work with. Without awareness of your inner workings, you invariably project your discomfort out onto the world. Do you always end up in a job where only you know what to do? Do you find yourself being hurt over and over in the same way by people with remarkably similar personalities? Are you always on the sidelines, waiting for something or someone better to come along? Are you continually unable to make decisions about your own life because things still aren't quite clear enough? A yes answer to any of these questions is a red flag. Any time you blame someone or something for your circumstance, an alarm should go off, and it's helpful to ask yourself what you may be ignoring.

Fear Causes Itself

Each of the three fears—passion, aggression, and ignorance—has a way of re-creating itself in our lives. Without awareness, we develop opinions and judgments that actually give rise to the very things we fear.

I once had a boss who fretted continually about how inept his employees were. It didn't start out this way. At first, we were charged up by the opportunity to work for him. He was a brilliant businessman and the company was successful. We felt confident about meeting his high standards because he had hired us himself. But we had no idea how high these standards really were because, just when we thought we might be satisfying them, they escalated. I found myself in tears a lot. If I was successful, my boss thought it was because I had taken his advice or simply gotten lucky. If I failed, it was because I just "didn't get it." If I took initiative based on my expertise, he faulted my iconoclasm. If I made sure to check in with him before acting, he shook his head at my lack of authority. I became truly inept very, very quickly. Without self-awareness on his part or superhuman self-esteem on mine, the environment of fear was unlikely to change. We each have something like this in our life, something that we think is happening to us but that really is emanating from us.

Experimenting with Spirituality

While in grade school, I began searching for anything that might explain—or at least lighten up—the sad situation I believed myself to be in, there in the dead silence of middle-class suburban life in the 1960s and '70s. Nothing made sense to me. I was a sensitive little girl and easily overwhelmed. Fear gripped my life from an early age. My days were spent strangled by shyness, and my nights were full of sleeping terrors. I had no idea how to discover why my life was the way it was, but I kept searching for answers. I was drawn to fairy tales, fables, and myths, thinking perhaps they would provide me with some clues. I read and reread my parents' child development books, hoping I could learn something from them. I read the encyclopedia; maybe the answer was hidden in one of its volumes.

At ten years old, I tried to write a psychology book in an effort to explain my point of view. I was desperate to communicate, to understand, but nothing was reflected back to me in a way I could recognize. Trips to the library were the focal point of my existence, and I found joy in reading about numerology, Celtic good-luck rituals, and the religions of Africa and Asia. At around age thirteen, I read the Bible. I came across it at a summer camp for Jewish girls, of all places. My counselor (who was not Jewish) had a copy on the shelf by her bed. I noticed that all her reading material seemed to be about something I had never heard of but knew I wanted really bad: *to be saved*.

My counselor, Cathy, was steady, tranquil, and comfortable in her own skin. I had never known anyone like her. At night, we sat out under the trees or in the gymnasium after everyone had gone to sleep and talked about the things that made us happy or sad, posited explanations for the difficult behavior of others, and imagined what a meaningful life might look like. I began to look forward to these nighttime discussions as I had never looked forward to anything before. For the first time, I was in an ongoing dialogue with another human being who thought about the same things I did, such as what caused certain feelings, what they meant, and why people did the things they do. But while my thoughts rose and fell in a dark, claustrophobic atmosphere, hers existed in a decidedly more affable climate. She was so relaxed. How did she do it? I wondered how someone could relate openly to others and remain steadfastly at peace.

I asked her how she managed to stay so calm, and after putting me off several times, she finally told me it was because of Jesus. She had accepted Jesus into her heart. She told me that, if I wanted to, I could do this too. Anyone could. I was shocked. I barely knew any non-Jews, and I certainly didn't know a soul who thought she or he was in a living relationship with anything more divine than country club membership. It didn't take long for me to realize that this—moving out of the suburbs and in with God—was what I longed for. If it was called Jesusville, so be it. Accepting Jesus as my personal savior had the added benefit of delivering a particularly creative and pointed message of rejection to my family, which at that age, I was really interested in doing. In this spirit, I accepted Jesus in an I'll-have-what-she's-having frame of mind.

Unfortunately, my first overt attempt to walk a spiritual path was a really bad experience. Once camp was over, I went home and informed my unsuspecting parents of my conversion. I suggested they might want to consider joining me; or else they could go to hell. They did not view my actions as simply an expression of teenage angst and were devastated, furious, and confused. Because there was no one to talk to about my wish to love God and no library book could help me decipher Jesus' instructions on my own, I was unable to figure out how to be born again—this time as someone nice and happy. I didn't have the skill to understand this path, nor did I know anyone who could explain it to me. I was too young to drive, and I couldn't take myself out to church gatherings or revivals, not that there were any among my neighborhood's carpooling moms and barbecuing dads. Instead, I locked myself in my room whenever *The 700 Club* was on television and tried to deconstruct what it was that caused those people to swoon with the spirit. I wanted to swoon too. But it was not to be.

My conversion was a huge struggle and a giant fiasco. It only alienated me more from family and friends, which made me feel even more miserable, guilty, and inadequate. Eventually, loving God and hating myself got twisted together, and the result was quite painful. I became more and more depressed and angry. My parents were shocked, bereft, and completely uncertain about how to relate to me, and I left home at sixteen.

Throughout these experiences of self-hatred, I repeatedly employed passion, aggression, and ignorance. I told myself many stories about what was causing me pain. I settled on one explanation after another for why I was so lost and messed up. When my old interpretations and justifications wore out, I struggled to find new ones. I believed that I could control my life through the way I chose to think about it, my ability to identify problems and craft solutions, and the speed with which I could determine the meaning of my own and others' behavior. This knack may have been effective in deciphering life on a certain conventional level, but until I acknowledged and looked into the reality of my own passion, aggression, and ignorance, freedom from fear eluded me.

The Antidotes to Fear

Finding a way to free yourself from explanations and cast yourself into the winds that blow hither and yon, not as an expression of surrender but as one of openness and courage, requires reconsidering the vantage point from which you view your own world. Contrary to what we might think, our will alone does not direct our life. Whatever does is some kind of mystery. The course of our life is determined by coincidence and chance as much as it is by what we think, feel, and hope for. What directs this course seems to be unknowable. Acknowledging this mystery is the very first step in fearlessness. When you make the moment-to-moment effort to detach from your ideas about what is going on and why so-and-so is doing thus-and-such, you let in a breath of fresh air. When you stop telling yourself new and better stories about the meaning of your life and allow yourself to *not* know, to let things unfold as they will: this is an opening to fearlessness. Instead of being crafted from scraps of perception and history, understanding presents itself to you as a whole. The moment you take your attention off your mind-chatter, you can hear the greater wisdom speaking to you through sudden inspiration, abrupt insight, and the ability to recognize patterns of activity or behavior. It takes courage to listen in this way.

We pay a very high price for holding on to our fears. Over and over, we alienate those we care about, and we don't know why. We create situations that are bound to disappoint. We lose out on opportunities because we're afraid of giving up the security of the status quo. We hold on to long-lost images of ourselves because they make us feel young, important, or affirmed. Most of all, we never get to figure out who we really are and what life is meant to be. In the grip of fear, our day-to-day experiences are held in an endless loop of self-recrimination, frustration, and confusion. When you live in fear, you never get to know the precious being that you are, and you're the only one who can ever do so. At the end of your life, the possibilities for your soul's expression in this lifetime die with you. This is too high a price to pay.

The place to start is by exploring your fears and touching base with their unique qualities and flavors through the practice of meditation. By sitting down, taking a deep breath, and having a good, long look at yourself, you can figure out where exactly to intercede in your thought processes to stop fear before it overwhelms you. You have the perfect laboratory for this exploration and for converting the energies of fear to fearlessness. The best path imaginable, the perfect one for you, is your everyday life, exactly as it is.

2

What Dissolves Fear?

WHAT ARE THE HALLMARKS of fearless people? Are they unhesitating about taking on new challenges? Able to stand on the ledge of a tall building or open their credit card bill without trembling? I don't think so. There is nothing reckless or hard-nosed about fearlessness. Nor is fearlessness the absence of fear, the ability to move forward with fear, in spite of fear, or the capacity to use fear as an energy source.

Tranquillity, compassion, and wisdom are the components of fearlessness, not power, control, and remaining unaffected. *A fearless heart is one that is able to remain open in all cases, retains mental and emotional flexibility, and never loses sight of anyone's humanity, dignity, and decency, including its own.* In this sense, fearlessness is an expression of balance and sanity. When we can tolerate ambiguity, space, and confusion without taking a defensive or aggressive stance, we are acting courageously. This ability is quite precious and, as mentioned, you already possess it.

When we trust and understand one another, it's not difficult to remain open and flexible. When we are confused, hurt, or shocked, it is much harder. Think about how hard it would be to remain open-minded and receptive to the one who broke your heart, took your job, or misspent your money. But it is possible.

The Antidotes to Fear

The three fears—passion, aggression, and ignorance—are what prevent this ability. Unlike psychological solutions that may suggest sophisticated stress-reduction techniques or development of increased assertiveness, the Buddhist antidotes focus on clearing up the misunderstandings that lead us to the poisoned mind state to begin with. Because the mind's natural state is tranquil (the opposite of passion), compassionate (the opposite of aggressive), and because it maintains perfect understanding (the opposite of ignorance), passion, aggression, and ignorance (the poisons) are viewed as simple confusion that can be cleared up by holding the proper view.

THE ANTIDOTE TO PASSION

Passion is a sign that we are confused about what brings contentment. When in the grip of this poison, we believe that whatever we're longing for—a raise, a boyfriend, a clean medical report—can actually make us happy. Of course, these things are great, sublime, and worthwhile . . . but can they truly make us happy? Perhaps momentarily, but not for long. Happiness that is conditional can always be threatened and therefore requires protection. Yet there is a kind of happiness that is effortlessly present at all times. This happiness comes from stopping the relentless search to fulfill our own needs. It comes from relaxing with things exactly as they are.

Working with the Passion of Heartbreak   For many of us, the most evocative experience of the suffering brought on by passion comes from romantic heart-break. If you've ever been cheated on, abandoned, or lied to, you know what I'm talking about. The anguish of longing can wake you up in the middle of the night and cause you to burst into tears the second your eyes open in the morning. You cannot draw breath without also inhaling the burning sensation of loss. The suffering brought on by heartache is monstrous. It obliterates every other emotion and destroys positive or even neutral energy before it can surface. Nothing can help you prepare for it. It's awful, it's luminous, and it completely takes over your life.

Yet heartbreak presents one of the most profound opportunities for spiritual awakening that one could possibly hope for. It destroys your point of view, which is incredibly valuable. You can no longer maintain your opinion of yourself, your ex, or the way your life was supposed to turn out. It's all gone.

I had my heart broken fifteen years ago, and I'll never, ever forget it. I'd certainly had failed relationships before and breakups that caused grief and sorrow. This was different. The pain ravaged my life. I filled dozens of journals. I lost ten pounds in two weeks. I made desperate, sobbing phone calls to friends in the middle of the night. I drove blocks out of my way to avoid passing a department store whose name matched the last name of his new girlfriend. Every night, I dreamt the same thing over and over again: he left me, he left me, he left me. Finally I moved to a new town as if I was shipping out with the French Foreign Legion. What was the meaning of this excruciating, endless pain?

I ran through explanations the way a cellist runs scales—over and over, each time with a slightly different feel, each time starting and ending in exactly the same place. "I can't believe this is really happening. He'll come back. No, he won't. Well, I hope someday he feels the pain I'm feeling. I hope he learns all the many terrible things about his personality. I gave and gave. I'll never feel desire again. He's scared of love. I'm too old ever to find love again. I can't stand thinking of him with her. I can't stand it. The pain is unbearable, I can't believe this is really happening . . ." It's possible to spend years with these thoughts. I did. They raced faster and faster, woke me up from drug-induced sleep, haunted me every minute of every day. This isn't an exaggeration. And you know what? None of those thoughts was true—or useful. None of them offered more than the most shallow sort of relief, and only momentarily at that. They actually distracted me from the possibility of relief and from my inner wisdom. I had no idea how to stem the tide of self-torture. Then, as sometimes happens when you're really desperate, I caught a break.

On this particular morning, I was taking out the trash (hmmm . . .) while thinking about the previous night's version of the he's-with-her dream. I began crying while dragging trash bags to the curb. I really thought I might just sit with the trash and hope to get thrown away too. Then, no joke, I actually heard a voice inside my head. It said, "Nothing is happening right now." I stopped. I looked around. It was true. Nothing at all was going on. This tsunami of agitation could not be located. I couldn't see, hear, taste, smell, or touch it. It was *not happening*. It was only a thought. And, I realized, my thoughts were killing me, not my broken heart.

Years later, when I became a Buddhist, I learned about something called the true nature of mind, spiritual teachings that help you to realize your natural perfection in a flash, all at once. For a moment you might feel completely relaxed and free from mental delusions and able to see the world as it is. Your mind is utterly clear and quiet. In this moment by the curb, I believe I received my first glimpse of the true nature of mind.

My pointing out instruction came from this voice that caused me to take my attention off my pain for one tiny second. In that second, I saw that everything was actually totally okay. No one was torturing me. No one was attacking me. I wasn't drowning. There was no pain, nor was there absence of pain, and nothing had been lost. The noise of passion subsided, and it was like when you suddenly notice that the TV is on even though no one is watching it, so you turn it off. In that moment by the curb, there was silence, and within the silence I could relax completely. I forgot why I was suffering because there was nothing there. Rather quickly, though, I slipped back into my regular, conventional viewpoint. However, I'm incredibly grateful to that voice, because it gave me a glimpse of what the cessation of passion feels like.

Try this: If you feel the sudden onset of any kind of longing—for an old boyfriend, someone else's job, a new car—try to remind yourself that this is a form of fear, because what you are really saying to yourself is that life is not okay without these things. Take your mind off the object of your longing and place it on the first thing you see. It could be a tree, your hands, the television screen, or your dog. Let your attention go fully into whatever you're seeing and try to list three physical attributes that strike you immediately: green, cold, scruffy, flat, sad-looking.

You could write them down. If that's not possible, list them in your head. Then think of three more.

This exercise is not going to solve all your problems, but it can give you a tiny bit of breathing space away from pain. These moments will add up, and eventually you will discover that you have moved beyond this particular craving. The key is to take your mind off your pain for a second.

The stronger your meditation practice, the more rapidly you'll be able to transfer your attention as you wish and have some dominion over your mental chatter.

THE ANTIDOTE TO AGGRESSION

The antidote to aggression (hatred, intolerance, and wishing others ill for any reason) is finding some way to regain a sense of openness so that you can act with compassion.

Aggression falls away when you are able to stop, breathe, and take a giant step back in order to enlarge your perspective on what is upsetting you. For example, you may be furious at your neighbor's dog for barking incessantly, until you see he's trying to tell you that your house is on fire, or you may feel insulted by a friend who won't return your calls until you learn she's been ill. It's always possible to take one more step back to enlarge your perspective on what makes you angry. If your compassion hasn't returned, you haven't stepped back far enough.

Compassion can be really, really hard when you think about all the people and situations that you find ridiculously infuriating. But acting compassionately doesn't necessarily mean being sweet and nice, or giving all your stuff away. In Buddhist thought, compassion is synonymous with skillful action, action that is rooted in seeing reality from the largest perspective possible. When you have the proper perspective, you know without thinking what the next right action is. If you see a child with a badly cut finger holding a Band-Aid he can't figure out how to apply, you patch him up pronto. It's obvious what needs to be done and doing it is considered compassionate. False compassion, or "idiot compassion" as it's called in my circle, would be, in this case, bursting into tears at the child's predicament or sitting him down for a lecture on self-care. These behaviors clearly lack intelligence and are an "idiotic" version of compassion, which is actually a very sophisticated skill.

Acting compassionately doesn't mean refusing to admonish people who make you feel terrible or sticking with hopeless situations because you feel sorry for the others involved. Putting an end to abuse or moving on from futile endeavors may be the most compassionate—and intelligent—thing you can do. (One good way of testing whether your motivation is rooted in skillful action or stuck in emotional sludge or codependence is to check for your sense of humor. If it's still there, there's a good chance that you are grounded and sane.)

Changing the Presets The other day my friend Josh was telling me about an acquaintance he ran into on a busy Manhattan street. They hadn't seen each other for a few years and began to catch up on families, health, and work situations. They spent a few pleasant moments discussing each other's holiday plans. Then they shook hands and went on their way. "It was no big deal," said Josh, "until a few moments later, I said to myself, 'Hey, I forgot, I don't like that guy!' "

What would their conversation have been like if Josh had remembered his previous judgment of this man's character or if his negative feelings had been retriggered, simply upon seeing the man's face? It would have been exactly like most of the conversations we have. We think we already know who will be fun to talk to and who will be a pain, who we can get along with and who we can't, or whether we can count on someone to measure up to our standards. We behave as if every relationship and every situation has been preset to its own channel.

We don't allow events or encounters to unfold, but we bind them to our view instead. We use our presets to keep people in their place, attack those we fear, and reduce our feeling of being threatened. Throughout the day, we surf from resentment of Dad's interference to the anticipated disappointment of low grades to trepidation about an upcoming doctor's appointment. Our presets also affect positive emotions: we expect to feel good after exercising, hope to enjoy meeting a friend for coffee later in the week, and anticipate the fun we'll have on our next vacation. This is totally natural, but these imaginings, even about very pleasant things, prevent us from being aware of what's really going on around us. The cycle is endless. We can't go to work, return a phone call, or buy a new pair of shoes without an extraordinarily complex series of expectations, judgments, hopes, and fears.

The downside to these presets is that the relationships we find ourselves in are the relationships we're having in our imaginations—not with any actual people. If you treat people as if you already know your feelings about them, you've actually shut them out completely, which could be considered a form of aggression.

An antidote to aggression is knowing how to create time, no matter how brief, between what you observe and feel and what you think. This gap is quite precious. It contains the ever-present opportunity to hear the truth, work with difficult feelings, offer what is needed, and change destructive habits. With it, you always have a choice about what you feel and how you act.

Try this: The next time you're by yourself doing something routine, such as driving to work, taking the subway, or walking the dog, take a break and instead listen to the sounds around you without tuning into any one in particular. Let your ears relax with all the sounds you can hear: cars, the chitchat of people nearby, the lawn mower next door, or the birds singing. Let your aural focus be open—take in all the sounds at once, without preference. Don't try to tune in to any one in particular. After a few seconds, return your attention to whatever you're doing.

Meditation trains the mind to rest in the present moment, in this sort of open awareness, which enables you to pay attention to who and what is around you rather than your thoughts about them.

THE ANTIDOTE TO IGNORANCE

A friend of mine who is just out of rehab has been telling me some of the techniques for maintaining sobriety. Besides attending an Alcoholics Anonymous meeting every day and finding a sponsor, the newly sober person keeps a journal to track her positive and negative emotions. "Relapse actually begins thirty days before the alcoholic takes a drink," my friend explains, "so we have to keep our eye out for the first sign of it and do something right away—call our sponsor, take a walk, journal some more—anything to break the momentum."

Using a journal to keep track of how you're doing is a great example of working with ignorance. It's not that my friend is an ignoramus because she can't tell when she's relapsing; she's simply unaware of when she gets on the slippery slope that will lead to a problem. Lack of awareness is, in some ways, the most dangerous of all the poisons. Passion and aggression can be countered, softened, or named. It's difficult to work with what you can't see or feel. Like my friend, though, we can begin to tune in to what may be lying just below the surface through patient review of our thoughts. This is exactly the skill taught by meditation. Generally, monumental realizations don't cut delusion, but the moment-to-moment commitment to work with thoughts as they arise does. In this way, observation is an antidote to ignorance.

Not Being Afraid to Look   Once I heard the American Buddhist nun Pema Chödrön tell this story about her teacher, the Tibetan meditation master Chögyam Trungpa Rinpoche. In 1959 Rinpoche and his attendants were fleeing Tibet to escape the Chinese invasion. One night they stopped at a monastery to eat and sleep, and at the entrance a fierce guard dog was chained to a post. He was barking and straining to reach them. Rinpoche could see the spittle spraying from his mouth. Carefully, the men walked around the dog, keeping as much distance from him as possible. With every step they took, the dog struggled harder against his restraints. Just before they got to the door, the chain broke, and the dog raced toward them. The attendants froze. Rinpoche began to run as fast as he could—toward the dog. The dog stopped suddenly, glared, and then trotted off.

When you take action in response to your fear, it alters fear's momentum. Deciding on a course of action (or paying close enough attention to sense that it's not yet time for action) reduces fear. This never fails.

Beyond Antidotes: Four Actions You Can Take Against Fear

Whether it's passion, aggression, or ignorance, there are four possible ways to take action in response to fear or agitation, four ways to move toward the object of your fear with intelligence. In Buddhism, these are called pacifying, enriching, magnetizing, and destroying. They can work alone or sequentially. It takes wisdom and training to recognize which action is appropriate at what time, and while they may seem obvious, in fact they are not.

PACIFYING

Pacifying is the act of trying to calm something or someone down. But this isn't done simply by shushing or saying that everything is going to be okay. In the context of working with fear, pacifying means opening to a situation without aggression, and without jumping to conclusions. It's like when you pick up the phone and your best girlfriend is on the other end, sobbing uncontrollably. Your first question is, "What's wrong?"

Naturally, you want to understand what's hurting someone you love. The simple act of inquiry begins to pacify her because someone is open to listening without judgment. It wouldn't be very helpful if you also burst into tears, began shouting guesses about why she's crying, or immediately offered specific consolation without knowing why she was crying. So when you come across an upsetting or frightening situation, first ask what's really going on, even if the conversation is with yourself.

ENRICHING

Once you've made your way into a particular situation through the action of pacifying, you can enrich it by offering assistance. Because you've opened to the situation in the spirit of genuine inquiry, you're more likely to understand what is really going on and, therefore, offer what is needed in a very simple way. In the case of your crying friend, after you find out what's troubling her, you could offer to listen to her all night long, suggest something helpful to read, or as my friend Steve requests when things are not going his way, send chocolate. (Which is almost never a bad idea.)

MAGNETIZING

Even when things seem hopeless, you can still magnetize options by completely relaxing with what you understand to be going on, whether or not you can "fix" it. From this relaxation, solutions or options became apparent, and because you're not filling the void with your own anxiety, pride, or denial, you can spot them. Then you may or may not choose to take action. For example, maybe your friend is still crying although you've listened to her for hours and made dozens of helpful suggestions while feeding her chocolate. Nothing seems to be working. At that point, all you can really do is wait. It sounds passive, but it's very wise. You wait until an option presents itself. Rather than confusing things by jumping up and down, or insisting on a solution that simply isn't appropriate, waiting magnetizes new energy and can bring about a novel solution.

DESTROYING

If all else fails, the fourth action is destroying. This does *not* mean telling someone off, ending a relationship, or burning down your office building. Here, destroying means you recognize what isn't working and stop doing it. For example, I've destroyed many parts of this manuscript during the course of writing it because the passages didn't work. (Much to my chagrin.) In this case, to destroy was the accurate call. In the case of your friend, if she is still crying about the same upsetting incident twenty years hence, you might consider telling her to buck up already. This would actually be a kindness, if it is done with *her* well-being in mind, not your own. And if you can do this for a friend, eventually you can learn to do it for yourself.

Remember: employing any of these actions without accurate understanding can create a bigger mess than you are in already. Don't necessarily try to use them, simply hold these four concepts in your mind and contemplate how they might be at work in the ways you approach what scares you.

Try this: The next time you notice fear arising, whether it appears as anxiety, melancholy, or anger, stop, grab a piece of paper, and write one short sentence that describes your fear. Start with the words "I'm afraid," and then scribble the first words that come to your mind, without regard for grammar or rationale. It could be something simple and clear, such as, "I'm afraid to check my e-mail because I've already got too much to do" or "I'm afraid about an upcoming conversation with my girlfriend" or "I'm afraid I have cancer." Slowly read your words over three times. Take a full inhalation and exhalation after each reading. Avoid any attempt at amping up or toning down your agitation. This simple way of spending five to ten open seconds with your fear gives you the experience of tolerating it. It's as simple as this. And you can always go back to freaking out later. . . .

Relaxing with Fear

Giving yourself the space to work with your fears by really letting them unfold can be quite unsettling. It's hard to differentiate careful consideration from self-indulgence. How do you know when you've leaned in enough, when you have hit on the exact cause of your fear and where it is located in your psyche? How do you relax enough to do this, in the presence of fear, that least relaxing of mind states?

There is no formula for figuring these things out, but here's some advice the Buddha gave to a sitar player when he asked, about meditation, was he working too hard, or not hard enough? The Buddha asked the musician how he tuned his instrument before playing. The musician said, "If I tune the strings too tight, they break. If I tune them too loose, no sound will come out. So not too tight and not too loose works best." To which the Buddha replied, "This is how you should hold your mind in meditation."

It works the same way with fear. If we immediately begin busying ourselves with explanations, solutions, and rationalizations, then we haven't allowed space for perspective to develop—we've responded with too much tightness. If we fail to look at what frightens us, if we blow it off or continually procrastinate about acknowledging our fears, we're missing an opportunity for self knowledge and skillful action. This is too loose. Fear invariably makes us do one of two things in response to this uncertainty and unpredictability: either we tighten up around it too quickly, and begin imposing structure and rules on something as yet fully defined, or we pretend that what frightens us is no big deal. We stop paying attention and space out.

In the end, of course, we can't banish our fear responses permanently. And life would actually be quite boring if we could. Fear heralds a boundary reached. Its energy is pointing you toward the next step along your unique and personal path—it's just in code. Hold steady to your heart's insights and let them mix with your everyday experiences. Follow the feeling of fear patiently and carefully, and it will teach you fearlessness. Most important, remember that you can hold your own fear fully, even when it feels impossible. You can be completely afraid without being afraid that you're afraid.

3

Meditation

AS YOU CAN SEE, fear gathers imperceptibly. It arrives via tiny, unexamined thoughts, and before we know it, we're entirely fogged in. Fear is dispersed in similarly small moments, by catching those arrows before they pierce us and turning them to flowers. Through meditation, we can learn to catch all the thoughts that arise in our own minds, examine them, and then make decisions about what they might mean or what actions to take, if any. Examining our thoughts this closely could feel strange and awkward at first. We're not used to taking ourselves this seriously. But eventually, doing so becomes second nature and a very healthy habit.

Most of us start a meditation practice out of dissatisfaction with some aspect of life. Over and over we keep on running up against our own sorrow or frustration—the sorrow of continually reaching but never quite grasping, the sorrow of age, the sorrow of loss, the frustration of screwing up in the same way again, or failing to achieve what we want. Without a way of dealing with everyday sorrow and frustration, stress builds. When we see a photo of a monk meditating serenely on a mountaintop or a beautiful woman sitting cross-legged in a field looking blissfully content, we can't help but think they look like nothing could ever upset them. How did they get that way?

But what way is that? Are they sitting there thinking, I am completely calm. This is awesome or There's nothing I can't handle; I feel so unafraid? Perhaps they are calm and confident, but what I've discovered is that calm doesn't necessarily mean placid, and confidence is not always about certainty. Meditative calm seems to come when you can fully experience any emotion, from joy to terror, without losing your center. Meditative confidence comes from relaxing and knowing that it's okay to open your heart.

Meditation Is Good for Your Health

Recently, it's come to light that meditation is a great stress-reduction tool. Neuroscientists, psychiatrists, and mental health professionals are now devoting considerable attention to measuring the results of meditation and pinpointing the effects it has on the brain. In fact, a small group of top scientists and medical professionals have been in serious dialogue for over a decade with His Holiness the Dalai Lama and others who have devoted their lives to meditation practice. Usually these meetings have been held privately, either at the home of the Dalai Lama in Dharamsala, India, or in the United States. In 2003 the dialogue was made public for the first time, and in November 2005 a second public dialogue took place. I was fortunate to attend both these events. Various world-renowned scientists, doctors, and researchers took the stage together with a cadre of accomplished monks from the East and West and Buddhists scholars. They discussed topics such as emotions, mental focus, cognitive control, and the relationship between stress and disease. The scientists presented research findings on meditative practices, and the Buddhists discussed the spiritual philosophy behind these practices. The scientists found that meditation practice has demonstrable effects on the parts of the brain that govern emotional and stress responses.

Dr. Richard Davidson, director of the Laboratory for Affective Neuroscience at the University of Wisconsin, has shown that longtime meditators have differences in brain circuitry from nonmeditators. He found that when you are upset—anxious, depressed, angry—certain regions of the brain (the amygdala and the right prefrontal cortex) become very active. When you're in a positive mood, these sites quiet down, and the *left* prefrontal cortex—a region associated with happiness and positivity—becomes more active. Davidson found that meditating monks had especially high activity in the left prefrontal cortex. One of the reasons this finding is so remarkable is that for a long time scientists thought the brain had a "happiness set point," which could not be altered. Study of meditators shows otherwise. This set point—your ability to be happy—can be raised. In addition, Davidson has found that meditators have increased frequency in electrical signals called gamma-band oscillations, which are associated with the ability to remain focused.

Our lives are full of stress and stressors. The acute stress that results from almost being hit by a bus is not the kind of stress that has a deleterious effect, though. This type of stress mobilizes your natural self-protection responses and capabilities. Chronic stress, however, can negatively affect health. Certain conditions are known to have significant relationships with chronic stress. An ulcer, for example, is caused by the presence of a particular bacteria in the stomach plus increased acid associated with stress. No stress, no ulcer. Other conditions with noted relationships to stress include heart disease, lowered immunity, diabetes, and asthma. There is evidence that chronic stress shrinks neurons in the hippocampus, a part of the brain involved in learning capacity, memory, and depression. But the hippocampus has the ability to regenerate if stress is discontinued. Research has shown that meditation reduces stress, giving benefit to the health of the body and the mind.

Studies of depression have shown that there are three contributing factors: brain biology, family history, and environmental factors, such as stress, loss, and trauma. The first two factors are not within our control. The third, however, is. We can't prevent loss and difficulty, but we can significantly alter our reactions to them. Zindel Segal, chair in psychotherapy in the Department of Psychiatry at the University of Toronto and a pioneer in mindfulness based stress reduction, has shown that MBSR participants are 50 percent less likely than other patients to relapse once depression is alleviated through medications and other therapies. This is because meditation teaches us, thought by thought, to alter our responses to stress, thereby increasing production of serotonin, a neurotransmitter that influences mood, sleep, and appetite. Antidepressants such as Prozac and Paxil, so-called SSRIs (selective serotonin reuptake inhibitors) increase serotonin. Meditation can have the same effect.

MORE THAN STRESS REDUCTION

Meditation can help you relax, alter your mood, and reduce stress, but it is so much more than a relaxation technique. It's actually your mind's natural state, so it's not something you learn, it's something you return to and rediscover. This can result in powerful self-knowledge and understanding of human nature. In this sense, meditation is a spiritual path, not simply a way to lead a healthier lifestyle.

There are many types of meditation. Some involve recitation of a mantra (a word or phrase that you repeat over and over), others rely on visualizing a particular image. In guided meditations, you are walked through a particular experience meant to evoke a certain mood or help you imagine yourself as the person you want to be. Each of these practices are a way of siphoning attention away from everyday thoughts and onto something that calms or steadies you. In the meditation practice I am introducing here, the object of attention will be the breath.

Shamatha Meditation

Breath awareness meditation itself is a powerful practice you could do for the rest of your life. It is as profound and sophisticated as you could hope for, yet it's also incredibly simple and accessible. If you choose to add other meditation practices, the ability to stabilize your awareness in the breath will be an enormous support.

The meditation we'll be practicing is called Shamatha, which means "peaceful abiding" in Sanskrit. This practice cultivates a composed inner environment, from which accurate insight and understanding can arise naturally. This form of meditation has been practiced for thousands of years by millions of people.

Shamatha, which I will explain in detail shortly, involves sitting on a chair or cushion and placing attention on the rise and fall of your breath. Your breath is always there, and it's always in the present moment.

As thoughts arise, you gently set them aside and return attention to your inhalation and exhalation.

You may think, Oh, I could never meditate. It sounds too hard, and I couldn't sit still for that long. Well, guess what? You're constantly meditating anyway, whether or not you've ever called it that. Your attention is going somewhere at all times and settling on something—but usually it's stuff like "I hate my thighs" or "My retirement fund is totally inadequate." In meditation, instead of taking our thoughts as the objects of our attention, we place our attention on the breath.

Shamatha Instructions

Find a quiet, comfortable place to sit. If you are planning to sit on a cushion on the floor, dress in comfortable, loose-fitting clothing.

Minimize distractions: turn off the phone, close the door, shut off any music or television.

Decide how long your meditation session will be. Ten to thirty minutes is great, although you can sit for as little or as much time as you like. If it's helpful, you can set a timer or alarm to indicate the end of the session. There are even clocks made especially for meditators. (The alarm mimics the sound of a meditation hall bell or gong.) I use a meditation timer that I downloaded for free.

Take your seat and review the points of posture: Sit on an even surface, legs crossed comfortably or feet flat on the floor (if on a chair); back is straight but relaxed, hands are resting on the thighs, palms down, eyes are open but soft, gaze is forward and down to a spot a few feet in front of you, mouth is closed but lips are slightly parted.

Before beginning the actual practice, remind yourself what you are doing, that you are about to meditate, that you will give it your all, and that during this brief time everything else can wait.

Now you are ready to start.

To begin, you'll need a chair or cushion that will allow you to sit up straight and a clean, attractive, and relatively quiet space. If you'd like to include in the space flowers, incense, or a particular photograph that inspires you, that's fine but not necessary. What's important is to select a place that feels pleasant, that you'd like to return to. If possible, choose an area that can become your regular sitting spot. You won't be playing music, so proximity to an audio system is not required. The setting should be simple and dignified.

Before you begin, take a moment and remind yourself of what you're about to do. You're about to meditate. My teacher, Sakyong Mipham Rinpoche, suggests actually saying to yourself something like "Okay, now I'm going to sit down to meditate. Everything else can wait. I'm going to devote myself to the practice fully." This way, you gather your mind and prepare yourself to practice.

Three Categories of Mindfulness

Meditation has three categories of "mindfulness": mindfulness of body, mindfulness of breath, and mindfulness of mind.

MINDFULNESS OF BODY

The practice begins when you take your seat. In fact, posture is so important that the Zen teacher Shunryu Suzuki Roshi described correct posture as the same thing as enlightenment! Posture is important because it allows energy to circulate freely in the body. Although it might not feel this way at first, the right posture minimizes physical stress and allows you to relax. In addition, many wisdom traditions (including Buddhism) think of the mind and body as connected. So sitting properly is important not only because doing so protect joints and muscles but because it enables the mind to relax.

Posture begins with finding a way to sit that allows your back to be straight. It should be not rigid or uncomfortable but relaxed. Some people can sit this way on a couch cushion or a regular pillow, and some prefer a meditation cushion (a pillow manufactured specifically for meditators; see "Meditation Resources" for a list of places that sell meditation supplies), and others prefer to sit on a chair. All of these options are completely fine.

If you sit on a cushion, cross your legs comfortably in front of you. If your hips are rotated too far forward or too far back, you'll feel stress in the legs, back, or shoulders. Find the right spot for you. If you experience knee or back pain, try raising your cushion, placing pillows under your knees, or moving to a chair.

If you choose to sit on a chair, find one that allows you to rest your feet flat on the floor. Sit forward on the chair until they do. If they don't reach comfortably, place a cushion or a few books under them until your knees are level with your hips and you are resting on your sit bones. (Your sit bones are the boney parts you feel against the chair or cushion when you sit up straight.) Your back should not be against the chair back.

Rest your hands on your thighs, palms down. Elbows are bent, arms and shoulders are relaxed.

Tuck your chin in a tiny bit to make sure the neck is straight. Let your jaw relax.

In this particular practice, the eyes remain open. Direct your gaze forward and down slightly, to a point approximately six to seven feet in front of you. Let your eyes be soft, resting back in their sockets. (Try doing this with your eyes right now. It feels really good.) You're not looking at anything in particular, just softly gazing at a spot in front of you, as if what you were looking at was meeting you halfway. Don't stare or strain.

Become aware of the space above you and the ground below you. You're in the middle, connecting heaven and earth.

MINDFULNESS OF BREATH

After settling into your posture, bring your attention to your breath. Place your attention at the tip of your nose and notice the breath as it comes in and goes out through the nostrils. You don't need to breathe in any special way, just let your breath be as it is. Note the gap that occurs at the end of the exhalation; then watch as the inhalation happens naturally. Follow the breath in and then let it dissolve into the space in front of you. Just like waves, the breath rides in and rides out. No one has to tell the waves how to do this. Your breath is exactly the same. Simply witness it. Go along for the ride.

MINDFULNESS OF MIND

You may notice that, within about one second, your attention drifts away from the breath. This is not a problem. Just bring it back. As soon as you notice that you've stopped attending to the breath, simply and gently return your attention to it. It's important to pay close attention, but it's of equal importance not to be upset or self-critical as you come back. Just gently drop your line of thought and return attention to the breath. If it helps, when you notice that you've become wrapped up in thought, simply label it "thinking" (silently) and return your attention to the breath.

In this practice, all thoughts are viewed as the same. It doesn't matter if one thought is incredibly kind and another is vicious. Great insights and petty whining are also just thoughts. As soon as you notice that you're thinking, no matter what the content, simply bring your attention back to the breath.

A common misconception about meditation is that it involves emptying the mind of all thought. It scares people to think they might have to try not to think at all. Nobody has to do this. In fact, you can't empty the mind of thinking. The function of the mind is to think, just the way the function of the eyes is to see and the function of the ears is to hear. You can't open your eyes or ears and try not to see or hear. You can't stop sight and hearing, and you can't stop the mind from thinking. Meditation is not about shutting thought off, it's about learning how to relate to them in a different way. Please remember that it doesn't matter how speedy, trite, meaningful, or vacuous your thoughts—gently let them go and return your attention the breath.

Dedicating the Merit

Traditionally, each meditation session ends with what is called a "Dedication of Merit." Dedicating the merit is an expression of hope that, should insights and emotions arise during meditation, they be used for the good of all beings (which includes yourself, by the way). This gives your practice a special depth and meaning and is one of the aspects that make meditation into a spiritual endeavor, not only a stress-reduction technique.

You can recite a traditional Dedication of Merit (see below for an example), or simply take a moment to wish that whatever energy has been generated through your practice could be used to create a more peaceful and joyous world. Your words can be as simple as, "I hope that what I'm learning will make me a better mother," or "I don't know how it could happen, but I wish that my meditation could help others." You can even dedicate your crankiness and irritation in this way by silently hoping that although it doesn't feel good to you, perhaps it's serving a purpose in some other way. Nothing fancy. My teacher, Tibetan Buddhist teacher Sakyong Mipham Rinpoche, says that not dedicating the merit is akin to forgetting to hit the save button before shutting down your computer. Sharing the benefit with others somehow ensures that the seeds of fearlessness and joy planted during meditation practice will take root and bloom.

LENGTH OF PRACTICE SESSIONS

Plan to meditate for about ten or fifteen minutes a day, either in the morning or in the evening. Try to meditate at the same time every day. Eventually you could build up to twenty, thirty, or sixty minutes. Use an alarm clock or timer to keep track.

A Seven-Day Program for building a meditation practice into everyday life is outlined in Chapter 8.

Obstacles and Antidotes

Each meditator has a different experience of the practice. Your meditation could proceed swimmingly in the beginning and become troublesome and confusing later. Or you could start out dreading practice and gradually warm up to it. But one thing that is for sure is that your practice will have ups and downs. How do you deal with the downs—frustration, boredom, and doubt—and avoid giving up on meditation?

Once I was teaching a weeklong meditation workshop at a resort in the rainforest of Costa Rica. It was a gorgeous spot, with lush vegetation and flowers overflowing in all directions. I could count at least twenty different birdcalls before I brushed my teeth in the morning. Guests could swim in either of two rivers running through the resort and then drink a fabulous piña colada made with fresh pineapple juice. Workshop sessions were to be interspersed with white-water rafting, horseback riding, and hiking. The participants were looking forward to a peaceful vacation in a beautiful place, one that would leave them refreshed, destressed, and armed with some meditation techniques to help carry these qualities home. For the first thirty-six hours, it seemed as if this was exactly what would happen.

My small group settled in quickly and earnestly and the first two days were great. But by the third day, the energy in the room felt pretty bad. It had gone from bright and hopeful at our introductory session to irritable and impatient. Wasn't meditating supposed to make us feel less stressed out? Why did it feel as if the opposite was happening? Was it supposed to be this hard? During a break on the third day, one of the participants came up to me with tears in her eyes and said, "This is excruciating. Please tell me I'm doing this for a reason. Why am I doing this again?" I knew exactly what she was talking about.

Sitting is difficult. I knew it could be tough through my own experience. Watching the discursive flow of mind can be embarrassing and irritating. All we want to do is distract ourselves. Who would want to sit around listening to this: Okay, I'm meditating now. I'm following my breath. Here it comes. There it goes. I think I'm meditating! My knee is really starting to hurt. My goodness, I'm getting old. I hope my bank deposit clears before the rent is due. Am I doing this right?

How can watching thoughts like these show the path to happiness? Shouldn't we be using this time more constructively? Wouldn't it be more helpful to picture something peaceful and lovely or repeat affirmations that could boost self-esteem?

Actually, no. Albert Einstein said, "We can't use the same mind that created our problems to solve our problems," and I really try to remember these words whenever I become frustrated with meditation. After a certain point, the harder we *try* to change the way our mind works—to stop being so angry, depressed, unfocused—the more confusing and irritating it is. It's more helpful to stop trying to talk ourselves out of painful feelings or force our minds to stay focused on "the positive" and simply relax by letting all our thoughts and feelings be exactly as they are. Over time, relaxing with your thoughts in this way significantly alters the way your mind works when you're *not* meditating.

Even if you accept that taking time to observe thoughts can be beneficial, it's not always easy to keep the practice up. The mind on which you're trying to get some perspective becomes irritated rather quickly by all this examination. Letting go of thoughts to focus on the breath can feel pointless. It's tempting to wiggle out of the situation as quickly as possible. "I have better things to do." "This is a waste of time." "It's not working." "This is making me feel worse." And so on and so on. Bring your meditation practice to these thoughts, as well: simply label them as thinking and bring your attention back. Do it over and over. Keep coming back. And, as I told my student, everyone experiences this irritation and frustration. Experienced meditators know that it takes a little time to settle down (it takes me fifteen to twenty minutes) and that you just have to sit with the irritation until it discharges on its own. Being frustrated is not a sign that things aren't going well. The solution to frustration in meditation practice is actually to *increase* your meditation time, and this is what I told my student in Costa Rica. Even five additional minutes will help. Otherwise, meditating is like trying to plant flowers in ground that hasn't been properly turned. You have to clear the debris away before anything new can take root.

In the twenty-five hundred years since people have been practicing Buddhist meditation, every imaginable obstacle has been encountered and analyzed. Being too busy, falling asleep, forgetting how to practice, and just plain feeling bored are some of the obstacles that have been defined and had antidotes prescribed.

Many kinds of obstacles and antidotes have been identified, but three of them—laziness, forgetfulness, and what is called laxity or elation—are most common.

Obstacle: Laziness

Not only can laziness be considered the king of obstacles but it's a complicated one. If all it took to vanquish laziness was to force ourselves to honor our commitments, success would be simple to achieve. But it's not that easy. Buddhist philosophy identifies several kinds of laziness, including these three:

REGULAR LAZINESS

Most of us are already familiar with regular laziness. You sleep late on Sunday morning, wake up at noon, lie on the couch with the newspaper or the remote, fall asleep again, and when you wake up at dinnertime, you still feel tired. You just can't seem to stay awake and shake the feeling of being super—weighted down. It becomes difficult to tell the difference between ordinary fatigue and laziness. Your mind feeds you lines such as, "You can do your errands tomorrow." "Meditation is not that important." And "You're better off just napping." This is the first type of laziness that we have to counter when beginning a meditation practice.

DISCOURAGEMENT

You might begin to think that your practice will never pay off or that you've tried as hard as you can and have yet to see any progress. Perhaps you have been meditating but nothing seems to change; the world keeps smacking you in the face. You feel tempted to give up. Feeling disheartened is considered a form of laziness in Buddhism. Both brand-new and longtime meditators encounter this feeling at some point in their practice: "I've been practicing for thirty minutes/days/years. When will my mind finally settle down?" But cultivating an undisturbed mind is not the point of meditation—returning to clarity no matter how ruffled you become, is. Don't let the Maras of discouragement rob you of your commitment to this effort. Remember that the benefits of meditation are taking root, whether or not you are aware of the moment they do so.

BUSYNESS

Paradoxically, having too much to do is also thought of as laziness. When you allow your schedule to become filled up with so many things that you can't remember your personal priorities, such as meditation and self-care, this is considered a form of laziness.

Because laziness is often the biggest obstacle to meditation, it has four antidotes! The other obstacles have only one solution each.

Four Antidotes to Laziness

TRUST

The first antidote to laziness is trust or faith. When I began reading about Buddhist meditation, I *knew* it was for me. Somewhere, sometime, you also had an insight into the value of spiritual practice, at least enough to have decided to give it a try now. Recalling this moment, reminding yourself of the feelings and insights that led you to the meditation cushion to begin with, can help combat laziness, just as remembering how good you feel when you eat well restores your resolve to choose fresh vegetables over cupcakes for lunch.

ASPIRATION

Aspiration can counter laziness. And genuine aspiration arises when you have personally experienced the benefits of meditation, or have seen how others have benefitted. Proof of the power of meditation can lead to the strength of conviction that cuts through laziness.

EFFORT

The third antidote to laziness is, of course, effort. This is not the kind of tight-jawed focus we bring to our desk when we have to work at something we have no interest in. This kind of effort has a quality of enjoyment that comes from deriving pleasure from your practice. I experienced this form of effort when I decided to try running as a way of keeping fit. At first, I genuinely hated it. I had no wind, no leg strength. It was winter in Boston, and I really don't like cold weather. One day after several weeks of forcing myself to try, I found myself on an icy street, cheerfully hopping over patches of ice and leaping over puddles with a sense of pure glee. I was so happy. I shocked myself. My stamina had caught up to my intention, and from that point on, running took on a different quality. I certainly didn't always *love* it, but my effort was infused with more than grim deliberation.

PLIANCY

The final antidote to laziness is called pliancy, which basically means that you've gotten to a place where your practice itself is strong enough to overcome your laziness. It's become a day-in, day-out habit that you can bank on, just as you know you're going to brush your teeth or drive your kids to school. You've reached a kind of critical mass and now it's just something you do. And just as you can't wait to brush your teeth when you wake up in the morning because it doesn't feel right not to, you want to practice more than you want to lie around.

Each of the forms of laziness will continue to appear, no matter how many years you've been meditating. The four antidotes are an arsenal of responses you can choose from to combat them. Over time, you'll become adept at knowing which one is called for.

Obstacle: Forgetfulness

Forgetfulness may sound like an unlikely obstacle—meditation instruction is pretty simple—but it happens all the time. It's a little bit like dancing. When my husband and I took tango lessons, we spent the first ten minutes of each lesson stepping on each other's toes, going left when we should have gone right and vice versa. It's not that we forgot everything we had already been taught, but at the same time, we did. Taking a few moments to mentally review the instructions before stepping onto the dance floor really helped. I've been meditating for over ten years, and still, every time I begin to sit, somewhere along the line, I have to remind myself to focus on my breath or not to lean back too far or I'll hurt my neck. I forget the instructions all the time.

Antidote to Forgetfulness

Review the steps of your practice as often as you need to. Spend time reading about meditation or otherwise familiarizing yourself with the instructions. Simply remind yourself every time you forget, without giving yourself a hard time. It can be especially helpful to do a short review before each meditation session. You could reread the instructions in this or another book on meditation, or you could listen to an instructional CD.

Obstacle: Laxity and Elation

Laxity and elation are flip sides of the same coin: both arise to distract the mind as it settles down. You may become drowsy or bored: this is laxity, another name for what you are experiencing when you get to your cushion, remember the instructions, actually begin to meditate, but find yourself falling asleep. The opposite but related problem, elation, is getting carried away by the sensations, emotions, or schemes that may arise as your meditation practice progresses.

When I reach the point where my mind starts to settle a teeny, tiny bit, thoughts, feelings, and sensations are invariably stirred up. Forgotten emotions arise, or I remember some task that I *must* attend to. I know I'm in trouble when I become overwhelmed by a tidal wave of "good ideas" and can barely resist jumping up to write them down. Sometimes, very strong emotions, such as sadness or anxiety, arise, and I find myself being carried off by them instead of breathing with them and making them part of my meditation. Others report strong physical sensations, such as warmth or electricity. It's easy to get caught up in the excitement of these unusual experiences. The problem with both laxity and elation is that they disturb meditative calm and clarity. They are both distractions.

Antidote to Laxity and Elation

Applying mindfulness and awareness by noticing all these things—your drowsiness, boredom, excitement, or great plans—labeling them as thinking, and returning to the breath is the key. Drowsiness will pass. Boredom will pass. Excitement will pass. Great ideas will still be there or will return later. In any and all cases, returning to the breath is an infallible antidote.

Essentially, meditation is the noble act of making friends with yourself. Breath by breath, moment by moment, you recover a sense of freshness, openness, and alertness. Through this practice, you cultivate a mind that is flexible and observant, a mind that knows how to remain present and receptive under all circumstances—which, as we discussed earlier, is the very definition of fearlessness.

4

How Not to Be Afraid of Yourself: Gentleness

Let us ride our horse of confidence.
Let us use our bow and arrow of genuineness.
Let us develop gentleness, so we don't have to destroy the world.

—CHÖGYAM TRUNGPA RINPOCHE

FEAR BEGINS WITH THE fear of self. Deep down, we're not convinced we're good enough—at anything. Self-doubt is our constant companion. Often, we don't know where this harsh self-criticism comes from. Our own mind? Parents? Teachers? Women's magazines? We are largely unaware of why we think the things we do. We each have particular self-criticisms that we like to con ourselves into believing. Thoughts such as I'm too needy, I'm not clever, I'm ugly/fat/old, I'm a loser, and It's all my fault can be our most familiar thoughts.

Whatever our choice of self-criticism is, we're constantly judging, weighing, measuring, and critiquing ourselves. We would never, ever apply such strict standards to others, holding back approval and affec-

tion unless extremely stringent guidelines are perfectly followed. Why are we too afraid to like ourselves
as we are?

In 1990 the Dalai Lama met with a group of Western psychologists, researchers, and leading Buddhist
teachers to discuss Buddhism in the West. Sharon
Salzberg, an American Buddhist teacher, asked him
about how to help students with low self-esteem, a
common problem that she had found extremely difficult to solve. How could she help her students with
their feelings of worthlessness and shame? The other
Western participants eagerly awaited the Dalai Lama's
response, because they had all encountered this im-
pediment among their own students.

The Dalai Lama turned to his translator. They began a lengthy, increasingly rapid conversation. Finally, it seemed the translator had succeeded in
explaining Sharon's question. When he understood,
the Dalai Lama was taken aback. He had never heard
about a person who hated himself. Why would you
dislike your *self*? He asked the participants if they
were certain their students or patients really suffered
from this problem. They assured him that they did.
They saw it in the people they worked with and even
in themselves. Incredulous, he pointed to each one
and asked, "Do you experience this? You? And you?"
They all nodded yes. He seemed genuinely shocked.
In Tibetan, there isn't a word for "self-hatred." In
the vast canon of Buddhist thought on the subtleties

of human nature and behavior, hating oneself had never come up.

But we can immediately understand what Sharon was referring to. Most of us experience the depression, anxiety, or anger associated with poor self-image, and we may go through some pretty elaborate rituals to prop ourselves up each day. I'm as good as my last phone call—if I had a pleasant or valuable interaction, I feel good. If things didn't go so well, if there was contention or distance, I think my world might be falling apart. Most people have their own measures for their worth or worthlessness, the car they drive, the school they attended, their job title, or even what they weigh.

Why do we feel so unlovable? And how, in an inner environment such as this, does one begin to cultivate self-acceptance, appreciation, and respect? How can we become gentle with ourselves?

Gentleness arises when you recognize your innate, limitless, and extremely powerful *goodness*. When you can understand how good, kind, and powerful you are, you can stop pushing and pulling yourself toward perfection as the only acceptable proof of self-worth. You are not the sum total of the perfect job, the perfect boyfriend, the perfect body mass index, the perfect sofa, the perfect what-have-you. How do I know that you possess this goodness? *We all do.*

Even if we can't identify it in ourselves, it's easy to recall a time when we were impressed by goodness in someone else. Perhaps you felt this way while reading the story of a saint, a hero, or even a regular human being who gave his or her all in the name of generosity and kindness. Maybe you felt it when you witnessed a mother tenderly drying her child's tears. Seeing how people greet each other or say good-bye at the airport, overhearing a particularly sweet exchange between husband and wife, or watching television and seeing victims of disaster being rescued can bring tears to our eyes. Watching a flock of birds move together in perfect connection or listening to an extraordinarily soulful piece of music can deeply touch us too. Our world is full of such examples of goodness.

The reason we can see the goodness of others is that we possess it too. You don't have to have been a very good boy or girl, or acted righteously and followed all the rules. Goodness is innate in all of us—if it weren't, you would not be able to feel it, just like if you weren't born with the capacity to speak, you would never recognize speech.

In Buddhism, this basic goodness is called Buddha-nature. It's not particularly associated with the historical Buddha, but it is what the Buddha already possessed that enabled him to transcend suffering, or fear. We each possess this enlightened quality, just like the Buddha. Buddha-nature is so innate and so precious that when low self-esteem was explained to the Dalai Lama, he asked, "How can people dislike themselves when they possess Buddha-nature?"

The Power of Gentleness

Gentleness toward yourself allows you to see your own basic goodness. When you clear away all the judgments, criticisms, assumptions, and beliefs by applying the mind of meditation to your internal experience, you discover that what is left is kindheartedness and joy. You can be patient with yourself, not because you earned the right through achieving goals or acting like a good person but because you possess a tender, beating heart that is always trying its best. In Buddhist thought, this is the sane and appropriate way to see yourself.

When we are angry, sad, or possessed by any burning emotion, though, it's easy to lose sight of our goodness. In fact, we may forget about it completely and instead get busy trying to make our sadness, anxiety, or anger *go away.* Explanations start pouring in: It's her fault, my fault. The world sucks. I'm a hopeless case. This will never work out. If only this hadn't/had happened. And so on. We throw our low self-esteem, anger at others, previous wounds, and general hopelessness on the fire. It's precisely here that meditation can help, after the moment we feel something difficult and before the moment we enflame it.

In meditation, the instruction is simply to be with your emotions, no matter how intense. Hold them with gentleness, the way you would a sad child. When a child is sad, you don't shake him and say, "What is *your* problem?" You don't ignore him and hope he'll go away. You can't really talk him out of it, no matter how brilliant your reasoning. You can just be there for him and with him. Difficult emotions can be dealt with in the same way. You can be this way with yourself.

Rather than diving into your feeling with great conviction and beliefs about how you came to have this emotion, you connect with its felt sense, which may sound weird, because aren't all emotions felt? Yes, but each one feels different. When I'm angry, for example, I feel heat in my chest and numbness in my jaw. When I'm sad, I have a sensation of waking up in mud; my body feels heavy all over, and not quite clean. Nervousness feels like diet soda is flowing through my veins. Each emotion has an accompanying feeling and, usually, a stream of self-talk or an inner tone of voice. The more you maintain your focus on the feeling of the emotion and not on the self-talk about how and why you feel it, the more quickly you'll return to balance.

Just as in meditation you notice thoughts, label them "thinking," and let them dissolve, you can notice your emotions, label them "anger," "frustration," and so on, and then let them go when you are ready to. You don't have to dig deeper and deeper into your own pain, which actually prolongs it. Instead, you feel the emotion fully, let it burn, and then, eventually, it burns itself out. Meditation teaches this ability to observe without becoming absorbed and losing perspective. This ability to "feel the feeling and drop the story," as the Buddhist nun Pema Chödrön counsels, is an extremely powerful example of gentleness toward oneself. You're not rubbing your face in your negative emotions, nor are you abandoning yourself.

We generally try to work with our negative emotions by analyzing them. This can be helpful in some ways. It can increase subtle understanding of what you feel and why you feel it. But, as so many of us have found, years of therapy aren't enough to change things definitively. By its nature, analysis is always reflective and always connected to the past. We may spend time pondering the meaning of a certain conversation, journaling about what we feel in certain circumstances, or talking an event over with friends or counselors, trying to deconstruct what happened. We may ultimately plan how to handle situations differently in the future, or we can make resolutions, murmur affirmations, or visualize how thing might turn out differently. So often, though, our plans and intentions dissolve in the face of real-life stress. There is an effective tool you can use in the moment—the mind of meditation. Through a meditation practice, you learn how to watch an emotion as you would watch a thought: you acknowledge it, notice its qualities, and watch as those qualities shift. Eventually, it all dissolves.

Meditative Outlook

Cultivating a meditative outlook doesn't mean you're never disturbed by waves of agitation or pain, it means that the waves, no matter how fierce, eventually break, wash up on the shore, ebb back out to sea, and you return to balance.

Try this: When you notice something has stung you—for example, a colleague criticizes your work, your partner is late for dinner, or someone cuts you off in traffic—begin to label your thoughts with the name of the emotion that characterizes them. "I hate it when he's late, he's always late, he promised not to be late," label that "frustration." "She is trying to sabotage me," label that "resentment." "I can't believe that jerk cut me off," label that "anger," then drop your attention down into your belly and pay attention as it rises and falls for three breath cycles. Then go back to being upset if you like. This way you teach yourself to interrupt the flow of emotion without turning it off. Instead, it plays itself out naturally.

There is always a price to pay for fear. When it goes on uninterrupted, when it is uncontained, fear can insert itself in the oddest situations and eventually take on a life of its own, beyond our control. Unexamined fear projected into the environment is probably the cause of violence, war, and fundamentalism. Violence toward ourself begins when fear causes us to settle for less, aim low, and tolerate gigantic messes in our life.

You can change this situation. You can't banish fear, but you can neutralize it in its tracks by creating a friendly and open relationship with it. Creating this relationship doesn't happen by simply thinking about fear, just as making a new friend doesn't happen by thinking about that person. You create a relationship with your fears and what causes them the same way you do with anyone: by spending time together and being receptive to each other.

We do so many things to escape from ourselves. Often that's the spirit behind the vacations we take, the books we read, and the substances we imbibe—and, just as often, it's the reason we enter therapy or begin spiritual practice in the first place. We don't like who we are or how we feel. We want life to be easier and more satisfying.

I don't know why, but so often the intuitive steps we take toward these things are in the wrong direction. We create our world in response to our fears. We don't like being sad or worried, so we read books that tell us how to feel in control and powerful all the time. We think we have been handed a raw deal, so to balance things out, we give someone else a raw deal. We make arbitrary decisions about what to have faith in because we're too scared to use our native intelligence. We run from ourselves. We will do almost anything to avoid looking closely at ourselves, which can evoke feelings of tremendous embarrassment and discomfort. Why are we so ashamed of ourselves?

Meeting Shame

I began practicing meditation in 1994. By early 1995, I had a meditation teacher with whom I met every Tuesday. We practiced together, and afterward we would discuss the practice. I asked questions about posture and technique, brought up things that confused or surprised me about meditation, and mentioned changes I had begun to notice in my emotional life. The more I practiced, the more sensitive I became to my surroundings. I felt more attuned to other people's energy and could sense their moods and inclinations more accurately. Because I learned to trust myself to remain relatively stable in the face of both happiness and disappointment, my openness to my own emotional intensity increased. I began to develop genuine emotional strength, the kind that is built on self-acceptance and without having to give myself pep talks. I began to feel more and more that the Buddhist path was exactly right for me. (Everyone has his or her own particular spiritual path, but most of us never quite identify what it is. I'm fortunate to have found mine. Buddhism isn't for everyone—there are many honorable spiritual lineages and, as I have said, you certainly don't need to become a Buddhist to reap these benefits.)

When I asked my meditation teacher how I might deepen my practice, he asked me if I was interested in formally becoming a Buddhist. "It's not that the credential is important," he said, "it's the intention." Making a formal commitment increases the intensity of any given situation, such as getting married or accepting a new title at work. "For some people, this [formally becoming a Buddhist] is very helpful. Others benefit more when they stay away from anything formal. But I think you may be the kind of person who responds to structure." He was right. I was already good enough at being spaced out and wild. Routine was actually comforting for me.

Becoming a Buddhist is called "taking refuge." One takes refuge in the Buddha (not the person but the idea of wakefulness), the dharma (wisdom, whether written or discovered through personal experience), and the community or sangha (your fellow travelers, which includes other Buddhists but also all of humankind). These are your three equally important teachers.

My instructor explained how it was done—he would read certain lines, and I would repeat them three times. He would choose a Buddhist name for me, which I could use or not. Some blessings would be made, and I would be a Buddhist. He said I would know if I was ready for taking refuge if the ceremony was an acknowledgment of an internal shift that I had already experienced. In some way, it would be just a formality. I felt that my internal shift was real, and so it would be genuine.

We fixed the date for my vow ceremony later in the month. I went home, made dinner, did some laundry, and went to sleep. I knew I had just committed to taking an enormous step, and as with most life-changing decisions, I had no idea what it actually meant.

The morning of the ceremony I awoke feeling

excited, scared, and uncertain. Would my life really change? Would I still be in charge, or would I have to cede control to the Buddha? What if I got a crappy name? What does one wear to take refuge, anyway? I showered, made some tea, and decided to wear jeans, a comfy sweater, and my weekend sneakers. After all, I thought, this is just a formality, not a big, fancy ceremony.

When I arrived at my teacher's house, he came out the front door to greet me wearing an elegant, finely made dark blue suit, with a perfectly starched white shirt and a silk tie. Everything about his expression, gait, and clothing telegraphed "This is important and I am taking it very, very seriously." He had never mentioned anything about formality, and I was ashamed that he had thought to honor my commitment in ways I didn't. He was clearly embracing the meaning of the refuge ceremony without apology or a false sense of significance. He was relaxed and focused. I was nervous and embarrassed that he was taking the commitment more seriously than I was.

It struck me that I was ashamed of my desires. Keeping everything casual was my way of holding back. Just seeing my meditation teacher in his suit made me realize all this in a flash. I wanted to turn back. I had made a huge mistake. I was about to take this important vow the way one signs up for a gym membership, zipping over the fine print and scribbling a signature to get the membership card. I cried for my lack of ceremony. I cried for my lack of understanding. I cried for the rips in my sneakers and the sharp crease of his trousers. I stood by my car, hesitant to walk up to his front door. He and his wife somehow knew exactly what was going on. I said, "I have no idea why I'm crying," and she replied, "Of course you're crying. You're raw and open." She was right.

My teacher's wife took me upstairs and directed me to their bathroom to freshen up, telling me I could use some of her lipstick if I wanted. I dabbed at my eyes with a cold washcloth, found a lipstick in a shade that I liked, ran my fingers through my hair, and walked across the hall to their small shrine room. We sat on cushions on the floor, facing each other. I felt the most curious sensation of relief and discomfort. After the short ceremony was over, they handed me a small scroll, which contained my new name. (Dechen Lhatso: Divine Lake of Bliss. Not bad.)

Before the ceremony began, I received my very first teaching as a Buddhist. Instead of coming to this ceremony to offer my good intentions, I had come to offer my shame. Instead of arriving with confidence, I had come slightly embarrassed about myself. I saw that I was afraid of making myself vulnerable to the commitment I was about to make. Like a groom who shows up on his wedding day in a tuxedo and sneakers, I was trying to make sure this was all still a bit of a joke. I didn't know how to take myself seriously without feeling pompous. Fearing looking too self-important, I took the opposite route and looked like I didn't care at all. I treated myself in this shabby way because I had not yet learned how to be gentle with myself.

When it comes to our own searching, our own longing, we're often a bit embarrassed. We don't know how to fully dignify our deep wish for happiness, so we live as if it doesn't matter that much. If we keep everything very casual, uncommitted, and safe, we don't have to worry about looking foolish. I won't declare my attraction to people until I know they're already attracted to me. I won't introduce new subjects into conversation with old friends without first testing for the humiliation factor. I won't wear this shirt, eat this food, listen to this CD, or take this trip without external validation from friends, family, or the media. Fear of who we are creates low self-image and shame, not the other way around.

We can cultivate a kind of simple gentleness toward ourselves. We can begin by relaxing. When you spot something you dislike about yourself, the tendency is to turn up the negative self-talk. I'm not suggesting that you replace it with positive self-talk. I'm suggesting that you drop self-talk as completely as possible and just relax. When you're in the grip of any negative feeling, whether it's depression, anxiety, or dread, try to stop talking to yourself about it. When you hear that voice in your head saying things like, "I'll never get what I want." "If only I hadn't done/said/thought certain things, all would be well." "I'm doomed to fail," stop.

Allow your awareness to drop away from your

thoughts and into your body. You'll immediately sense some physical sensation. Pinpoint where the sensation is in your body. Such thoughts are always accompanied by a physical reaction or manifestation. Perhaps your shoulders are hunched up, your belly is tight, or your breathing shallow. As soon as you notice where the tension is, relax it. If you can't relax it, relax everything else around it. Relaxing around tension is common in yoga practice. When we feel discomfort in a certain pose, the tendency is to tighten up all over. If your hamstrings ache in downward dog, your neck muscles may tense. If you're afraid you'll lose balance in tree pose, you may grip the ground with your toes. These attempts to gain control aren't helpful. The instruction in yoga is the same as it is here: relax around the holding. Be gentle with yourself. Yes, one part of you may be uncomfortable, but you can still relax everything else.

Try this: Make a tight fist with your right hand. As you do, notice if your shoulder or jaw has also tensed up, or if your eyes are squinting. Perhaps your thigh muscles have clenched or your neck has strained forward slightly. But your shoulder, jaw, eyes, thighs, and neck are not needed to make a fist. Relax them all without relaxing the grip of your fist. It's possible to hold tension in one part of your body without allowing other muscle groups to get in the picture. You can do the same thing with your thoughts. If you feel angry about all the other times you didn't get what you were hoping for, let the anger be localized only. Relax everything else.

Like a mother being handed her newborn child, connecting with our own souls is equal parts raging power and sweet tenderness, inseparable from each other. A mother would use that power to stand between her child and an oncoming car. Her tender feelings would lead her to do so; her power would support those feelings without hesitation. So in love, there is also great capability. When you can extend this love toward yourself, when you allow for the subtle unfolding of your own vulnerability, you can develop friendliness toward yourself, stop living your life as an ongoing self-improvement project, and relax.

The practice of meditation teaches you to relax your mind, thought by thought. You don't have to get caught up in any particular line of thinking. In relaxation, something quite wonderful develops. Tenderness and warmth rise to the surface effortlessly. The gentleness you extend toward yourself can now include others. When the heart knows itself to be secure, it freely and gracefully turns toward others.

5

How Not to Be Afraid of Others: Delight

AS I WRITE THIS, I'm sitting in my room in a spiritual retreat center in western Massachusetts. The air is cool and dry at 7:00 A.M., and although the room is monastic in size, the double bed is cushy and the walls are freshly painted a soothing sage green. It's spring in the Berkshire Mountains, and white, orange, and yellow tulips are just about to blossom everywhere. All around, center guests are doing their early morning stretches and meditations. When they arrive in the dining hall for silent breakfast, they'll find steel-cut oatmeal, hard-boiled organic eggs, and freshly baked kamut-sunflower bread. After breakfast, they'll move to the program rooms for the classes they've signed up for, classes with names such as "Getting the Love You Want," "Living the Questions," and "The Art of Extreme Self-Care."

The first time I attempted a program like this, more than ten years ago, I sat in the seat closest to the door. I wanted to be able to slip out silently if it was too weird, cultish, or nauseatingly New Agey. I watched my classmates make their way to their seats. Two fortyish women with hip haircuts walked in together, laughing. A graying man in spandex bike shorts took a seat next to them. A young woman with a nose ring and dreadlocks, reeking of patchouli, plopped down next to me. Eventually, all twenty or so participants were seated.

As we waited for our program to begin, I looked around. The laughing women seemed superficial and suburban. I could never have anything in common with them. The graying man, I was sure, had come to pick up women. Why did he have to wear those shorts? Yick. I was already planning to avoid partnering exercises with the nose-ring girl; I didn't want to hear her go on and on about how her parents hated her tattoos or how hard it was to be bisexual. In fact, I noticed, every single person in the circle looked like a loser. How could I share my inner thoughts with *them*? This was a giant waste of time and a huge mistake.

A few days later, the program was over, and as I gazed around the circle at my fellow students, I couldn't bear the thought of leaving them. The two suburban women, the graying man, the nose-ring girl, and I shared a long, lingering lunch together on the last day. There were many hugs and meaningful gazes. As we said good-bye, we cried. During the program I had developed a willingness to jump into their lives and help in any way I could. I felt so much love for them.

How were these people transformed from threatening losers into my new best friends in three short days? It was simply because we dropped our preconceptions, and talked. We took a chance, spoke from our hearts, and got to know one another for real. I learned that the two women had been best friends since grade school, and one had just been diagnosed with breast cancer. One friend was going to move in with the other while she went through treatment to take care of the children. The man who sat next to them had fallen deeply in love with another woman while his wife was pregnant with their second child. Whose heart would break first? Probably his. The young woman with dreadlocks had been sexually abused as a child, and the repercussions of this violation were threatening to destroy her first real love affair. Should she tell her lover about the abuse? What if she couldn't handle it and left her? Each member of the group had a very real, very powerful story of difficulties endured. Each was making the best effort he or she could to go on with life as a whole, healthy person. If there were twenty of us in the group, my heart broke nineteen different ways. By the end, each person's face seemed marked by sincerity and good-heartedness.

My own fears and insecurities had prompted me to judge these lovely people as losers without my ever having heard a peep out of them, without my knowing them at any level. Since then, I've noticed that I repeat this behavior every time I'm in a room with people I don't know. Her haircut is pretentious. He looks pompous. She is self-absorbed. And I'm sure they are thinking whatever negative thing they can come up with about me. We all do it. How can we step out of this loop? The practice of meditation helps you get free from your immediate negative reactions, which are fear-based. Instead of being judgmental, you can become inquisitive about other people.

Delight comes from replacing criticism with openness and genuine curiosity about others. Because you know how to recover emotional equanimity, you can take more chances. It's not necessary just to listen endlessly to whatever people say or to like them no matter what. But because our typical first response to others, known or unknown, is to retract our energy and wait until general trustworthiness is proven, we remain closed to those we encounter, even to our own friends and family, until some type of safety is established. We can relax when we know that this person thinks the way we do or can be counted upon to act according to our expectations. When we engage with someone we're unsure about, it's usually because she or he has something we want. We close our eyes, grit our teeth, and hope for the best.

Meditation is the practice of meeting whatever comes to us with equanimity and openness. If the Western ideal is "tough on the outside, soft on the inside," the Eastern approach is to become soft on the outside and tough on the inside. We can soften and be open to others because we have the discipline to bring ourselves back into balance. We can do this because we have some measure of trust in our own and others' basic goodness.

Try this: The next time you encounter someone who is angry or aggressive, and you're so scared you want to run away or fight back, try this: slow down. Slowing down in the midst of an argument or some other difficult episode is totally possible. When someone is yelling or criticizing or otherwise acting in a threatening way, let your attention go out to him. Rest your attention on him and for a few seconds try to take your attention off what he's saying. Instead, see if you can get a sense of how quickly his energy is reviving. If his energy was music, what would the tempo be? Connect with that tempo, and as you do, notice how your own body tenses or accelerates to meet it. As you connect with that tension, simply slow down your breathing until you feel you have returned to your own body rhythms. The idea is to find yourself first while someone else's energy is pulsing around you.

You can practice this by listening to music. Put on something noisy and raucous. Pick out the beat. Tap your foot or fingers in time with it. Then sit still and listen again. Start slowing down your breath as you are listening. Notice how the music is still there, playing and ricocheting at its own speed, and you are slowing down in the midst of it. Cultivating this technique teaches you to remain mindful and connected to yourself and your own agenda even when another's threatens to overwhelm you.

No Need to Wait

When it comes to caring for others, we usually wait for them to inspire some kind of genuine affection in us. Otherwise, it seems fake to offer our friendship. Unfortunately, this attempt at authenticity creates a mutually defensive air. Sometimes there is nothing wrong with a little forced caring. When I moved to Boston from Texas, I was shocked at how unfriendly people seemed. If I went into a store, the clerk wouldn't say hi. If a driver tried to enter heavy traffic, no one slowed to make it possible. If I went out for a walk in the morning, my neighbors did not wave to me. When I began telling my Boston friends about how much friendlier Texas was, they would look at me quite earnestly and say, "Yes, but they were being fake." So what? Pretending to be nice can be just fine. It's a great beginning.

Ultimately, the most effective way of dispelling anxiety between people, whether it's you and your mother, boyfriend, boss, best friend, or a complete stranger, is being friendly first. You might have to fake it initially, but do it anyway. There's a much better chance of finding a genuine way to extend yourself if you simply try to, even if you don't feel like it. Think of it as you would learning anything new. You must practice it before you can master it.

Beyond manufacturing a connection with others, there are ways to foster that connection that are surprisingly beneficial to you and the people around you.

Four Kinds of Friendliness

In Buddhist thought, there are four categories of friendliness, which are based on the notion that you can open your heart to anyone in a way that is very empowering for self and other. In other words, the love is there, you simply need to discover how to tap into it—and you don't have to wait until a person earns your affection before taking them into your heart. It can work the other way. First, you take them in unquestioningly and from this, acceptance and genuine affection arise. When you stop and take a look, you can almost always find a teeny, tiny spot of tenderness in yourself and it can be used as a spark to ignite authentic friendship. The Buddhist teachings say that you already have an unlimited reservoir of such friendliness to draw on. In fact, the traditional name for these qualities is the Four Immeasurables. They are expressed in these four lines:

May all beings enjoy happiness and the root of
    happiness.
May all beings be free from suffering and the root
    of suffering.
May we never be parted from the great happiness
    free from suffering.
May we dwell in the great equanimity, free from
    passion, aggression, and prejudice.

These lines are saying that you can extend kindness
to everyone, without judgment. The first line refers to
the concept of loving-kindness—simple kindliness toward all. The second line is an expression of compassion. "Sympathetic joy" is the ability to take delight in
the happiness of others, as indicated by the third line.
Equanimity, referred to in the final sentence, is the
ability to stabilize the heart in openness.

LOVING-KINDNESS
May all beings enjoy happiness and the root of happiness.

Loving-kindness is viewed as a practice, not an emotion. Through this practice, you can feel kindness toward anyone, under any circumstance, without acting
like a saint or giving in all the time.

Maitri is the Sanskrit word for "loving-kindness."
Loving-kindness doesn't mean acting nice even when
you really, really don't feel like it. Maitri meditation
teaches you how to generate loving-kindness under any
circumstances, no matter how you feel. It can be prac-

ticed in the same way as Shamatha meditation—in fact, practicing Shamatha for a few minutes before and after Maitri is recommended—but it can also be practiced on the bus, in bed before falling asleep, or while taking a walk. You can practice Maitri sitting on a cushion in meditation posture or lying down on the couch. Your eyes can be open or closed.

During the practice you offer unconditional friendship to yourself, to a loved one, to a friend, to a stranger, to an enemy, and finally to all beings. You call each one to mind and then wish these things for her or him:

> May you be happy.
> May you be healthy.
> May you be peaceful.
> May you live with ease.

It is very important to begin the practice with yourself. Bring an image of your own self to your mind's eye. Think about how hard you work for happiness. Allow yourself to feel the strength of your efforts. Sometimes it is tempting to skip this step because it can seem awkward at first to wish yourself well in this simple way. It can feel a little sacrilegious or as if you're being a narcissist or something. But it's beneficial to practice simple acceptance of yourself and your wish to be happy. You can then begin to feel compassion for yourself. The Buddha said, "You can search throughout the entire universe for someone who is more deserving of your love and affection than you are yourself, and that person is not to be found anywhere. You yourself, as much as anybody in the entire universe, deserve your love and affection."

From this basis of loving-kindness toward yourself, move on to your loved one. You can choose your spouse, a child, or a pet. You don't have to work to generate love for this being, you simply think of him or her and love is there. If no one makes you feel this way, you can imagine an admirable character from a book or movie. When you think of this person, you know how hard he or she has tried to be happy, and you wish that person this happiness completely.

The person you choose as friend can be anyone who has shown kindness to you. It could be your best girl-friend, a teacher you had in fourth grade, or a doctor who took care of you. This person too wants to be happy, and you can wish this for her or him.

A stranger should be someone about whom you have no feelings, positive or negative, such as the supermarket cashier or a person you sat next to on the bus. You may not know this person at all, but you can be certain he or she too is trying to find happiness. Although you may not have a sense for this person's efforts toward achieving happiness, you can wish him or her well simply because they, like you and your loved one, have joys and sorrows and are struggling in their own way.

Then choose an enemy, someone who has hurt or angered you. It doesn't have to be the worst person you've ever known, although it could be. Pick someone with whom you've argued or who has disappointed or caused trouble for you. If there is no one like this in your life, you can choose a historical or public person. Bring this person's face to mind, just as you did with the others, understanding that she or he just wants to be happy too. See if you can touch base with this understanding. From this place, wish for his or her happiness. It is no problem to do this for a loved one, but for whomever you've visualized as an enemy (your ex-spouse, a backstabbing colleague, a politician, someone you really detest), it becomes challenging to offer happiness. But that's the whole point. It can be extremely healing to offer happiness to someone you ordinarily wish ill—even just learning that doing so is possible is very inspiring.

Finally, offer your good wishes and tenderheartedness to all beings. Everyone, every single creature, is trying to be happy, to find warmth, to get enough to eat, to create a home, and to protect those who are dependent on her or him. Animals, insects, and birds also exhibit these behaviors; all beings do. You can take them into your heart and wish them well.

Loving-kindness in Action   I learned how to offer loving-kindness to someone I disliked when my husband and I were in the worst, most protracted period of disconnection we had ever experienced. We fought constantly. We had had lots of fights over the course of our relationship, but these were different. They were about nothing. Every single thing one of us did or said caused grievous insult to the other. We couldn't get out of it. We tried everything—talking, ignoring each other, having sex, avoiding sex, venting our feelings; it got to the point where we were about to present each other with charts and graphs. I kept waiting for this particular front to blow through. But nothing changed. Every day felt cold and sad. We were occupied by thoughts such as My spouse is a jerk—how come I didn't know? This person will never make me happy. I'm doomed if I stay here. We were both at our breaking points.

At around the same time, I was reading a book about Maitri practice. As I did, I cried every time the word *loving-kindness* appeared. I was longing for this! But I seemed incapable of offering it or receiving it.

My husband, Duncan, and I had done loving-kindness practice before, putting each other in the place of the loved one. I wondered if there was any way we could attempt this practice in the midst of our conflict without further annoying each other. I proposed we give it a try—maybe attempting to think loving thoughts about each other would turn our situation around. As we sat down in our meditation room, I thought, This guy is not my loved one—he's barely a friend. He's more like a stranger right now. No, wait. He's my enemy. I suggested we place each other in the role of enemy to do the practice. We both breathed a sigh of relief, because this was the truth. We couldn't possibly pretend to love each other. We began.

When I thought about a loved one, I imagined Duncan's son. I silently sent him the wishes: "May you be happy. May you be healthy. May you be peaceful. May you live with ease." Then I sent them to a friend (my sister), and a stranger (the lady behind the dry cleaner's counter). To each of these people, I sincerely wished happiness, health, peace, ease. Then it was time for my enemy. I brought Duncan's face to mind. Although I wanted to slap it, somehow I located the intention to wish him well, even though I wasn't sure I could actually do it. So I wished him happiness (or wanted to). I wished him health. I wished him peace. I wished for his ease. At the end of the practice, we opened our eyes and looked at each other. Nothing had changed. We barely mumbled good-bye to each other as we walked out the door, slammed our car doors shut, and went to work. That evening, it seemed as though we were still stuck. Then Duncan offered to get me a fork when he noticed I had forgotten to bring one to the dinner table. I poured him a glass of water. I looked at him, and he looked at me. We breathed in and out. It was over.

Duncan and I never figured out why we were so irritated with each other. No pathology was discovered. No childhood wounds were healed. No promises were made, and neither one of us apologized. Instead of working through our problems according to a linear strategy, we were able to rely on the practice of loving-kindness to reopen our hearts to each other. It was that simple. When you're angry or estranged, it may or may not help to dissect the reasons why; it certainly won't help to do so when you're still angry. But through Maitri, you can find a way back to your own natural tenderness, offer it to each other silently, and let the well of loving-kindness fill up again.

Maitri Instruction

Remember, in this practice you touch your own natural tenderness and begin extending it out in wider and wider circles, first to a friend, then to a stranger, to an enemy, and finally to all beings. This practice can be done seated in formal meditation posture, sitting in an easy chair, or lying in bed. Eyes can be open or closed.

Begin with yourself. See yourself in your mind's eye and think for a moment about how hard you work to create happiness for yourself and others, make a living, express yourself, accomplish something in this life. You make so much effort. Sometimes it works and sometimes it doesn't, but somehow you keep trying. With these thoughts in mind, allow yourself to wish for your own happiness. Say to yourself, silently:

> May I be happy.
> May I be healthy.
> May I be peaceful.
> May I live with ease.

These phrases are used in traditional Maitri meditation practice. If these words don't feel quite right to you, you can substitute others.

Let your awareness of yourself and your efforts to be happy fade. Bring someone you love to mind, someone who, when you think of him, causes your heart to soften. It could be a parent, partner, child, or dear friend. If you can't think of anyone who makes you feel this way, bring to mind a pet or a character in a book or movie who has moved you. Think about how hard this person has tried to create happiness, how he has struggled and worked. Then send this loved one the loving-kindness phrases:

> May you be happy.
> May you be healthy.
> May you be peaceful.
> May you live with ease.

Next, bring to mind a friend. It doesn't have to be your very best friend, although it could be. This should be a person who has been kind or helpful to you or let you lean on her. Think about her efforts to be happy and send the phrases to her.

After this, call a stranger's face to mind and wish him well too. It's totally possible to wish someone well when you don't know him.

Now think of an enemy—someone who has wronged you. Let your enemy's face come to mind. Know that this person too is just trying to be happy, no matter how strange her attempts may look to you. Send her the phrases, and try to really mean it.

In the last stage of the practice, let any particular person go. Realize that all the people in the world have friends and enemies, people they love, and those they are indifferent to. Each of these people, every single one, is trying to find happiness. All creatures are. Take a few minutes and wish that all beings could be happy.

Let the practice go, and relax for a few moments before getting up.

One of the great things about Maitri is that you can flash on it and extend it anytime. Walking down the street, you could extend it to a stranger. You could offer Maitri to a friend who is upset, on the spot. You could offer it to yourself before an important meeting or a scary doctor's visit.

COMPASSION

May all beings be free from suffering and the root of suffering.

Compassion arises when you contemplate someone else's pain without worrying about how it might affect you, without a personal agenda. When you see another person suffer, you automatically want to free her or him from that suffering, no matter what. We are all capable of this.

When I was about seven years old, I had been given a kite to fly during our vacation at the beach. My father taught me how to hold it, how to cast it into the wind, and what made it dip or soar. He held on to the kite with me until I was ready to fly it on my own, and then he let go. I ran up and down the shoreline by myself, following the currents of the wind. He could see how overjoyed I was. He was so touched by my delight. Suddenly I lost control of the kite, and it blew away. I ran down the beach trying as hard as I could to catch it as it blew higher and higher. I stopped only when the kite was no longer visible. Many years later, my father still remembers how torn up he was by the look on my face. If he could have flown up in the sky to retrieve the kite for me, he would have.

My father didn't feel my pain by sitting down and considering it. His compassion just happened, on the spot, beyond theories, values, or beliefs. A child's pain finds its way to a parent's heart. The door is simply open.

Maitri cultivates this sense of kinship with all people. When you do this meditation, when you practice holding your heart open to everyone, from your loved ones to your enemies, you are training to feel for all beings the kind of compassion my father felt for me.

Sometimes, though, it seems impossible to feel compassion for certain people. You can't force yourself or try to feel it on principle. Instead, you can simply think the sentence "May all beings be free from suffering and the root of suffering." You can even do this before beginning or ending Shamatha meditation (see Chapter 3), as a regular part of your practice. Spend a few minutes contemplating the words. Don't analyze them; simply let them be in your mind and watch what thoughts and feelings do or don't arise. Turn your attention to this sentence as you would to your breath. When awareness strays, bring it back to the sentence.

SYMPATHETIC JOY

May we never be parted from the great happiness free from suffering.

Suffering is not the only thing that can cause your heart to open spontaneously. This opening can also occur when we observe someone else's authentic happiness. Anybody who has ever cried during a soft drink commercial or at a wedding has experienced sympathetic joy. When my husband proposed to me over dinner in a restaurant, the lady at the next table burst into tears before I did. Something inside us is deeply touched by meaningful moments, no matter who experiences them. There is a spontaneous upwelling of joy for others.

When others are happy, we have the capacity to feel that happiness as if it were our own. We're not just happy for them, we feel happy ourselves. As you learn to feel compassion at the pain of others, you're also learning to feel pleasure at their joy.

EQUANIMITY

May we dwell in the great equanimity, free from passion,
aggression, and prejudice.

When I was working on this book, I read a news report about Al-Qaida's vow to carry out "major attacks" in light of the death of Abu Musab al-Zarqawi so that Osama bin Laden "will see things that will bring joy to his heart." My mind started spinning. What does this mean? Is it true or is it a bluff? Will it be here, in Iraq, or somewhere else? Tomorrow or next year? Why, why, why must we hate this way? How can we make it stop? What can possibly put an end to the dreadful momentum of hatred? Has it ever been this widespread? How can *I* make it stop? I can't. Forget it. I can't.

These thoughts flashed through my mind in less than a minute, without moving an iota from my couch. Simply by reading these words of threat and hatred, I was filled with dread, confusion, hopelessness, and shocking grief. I wanted to *do* something. I wanted to join hundreds of antiwar causes, write an article on how hopeless violence is, burst into tears, or go back to bed. Some or all of these might have been decent ideas. But in the grip of fear, I couldn't tell what made sense.

Unfortunately, I don't have a nice Buddhist way of saying, "Well, it's really all okay and this violence and hatred will make us better people." It isn't, and it won't. When I don't have any solutions and can't sense the right next action, I become frantic. I was in danger, not just of feeling scared, but of acting scared: fighting back, falling apart, sticking my head in the sand, or wishing violence on others. These are the opposite of the qualities the world is calling for right now, but I couldn't come up with any other options. There was nowhere to go. In the meantime, all I could do was not fall apart, which is an inadequate way of describing equanimity.

Equanimity comes from taking the biggest perspective, having the deepest understanding, and holding the longest view. It's like when someone cuts you off in traffic, and as you turn to cuss at him, you see it's your neighbor taking his pregnant wife to the hospital. Anger simply evaporates because you now understand the basis of his actions. When you back up far enough to comprehend fully the nature of the situation, equanimity is invariably restored.

Equanimity is, in some ways, the cornerstone of all forms of friendliness. Without equanimity, I find that I can offer loving-kindness, compassion, and sympathetic joy only to people I already like. But with equanimity comes the ability to offer these feelings to people I don't like, which is quite powerful. Equanimity allows you to open your heart to anyone, to stabilize yourself in this openness, and to become a source of transcendent kindness.

Meeting Relationships with Loving-Kindness

You would think that offering loving-kindness would be easiest with the person you are in love with, but it isn't. Examining loving-kindness in the context of romantic love can point out just how complicated it is to put all these forms of friendliness into play. Loving-kindness isn't a matter of sweetness and light—it's a deeply rooted commitment to seeing life (and lovers) as they are, *not* how you wish them to be. The more intimate we are with someone, the harder it is to do this.

I learned some of these lessons a few summers ago when I went to a monthlong meditation retreat in Colorado. At dinner on the first evening, I struck up a conversation with the guy sitting next to me. He looked to be in his early sixties and was a longtime student of Buddhism. We told each other a bit about ourselves, including our work and our relationships. He was thinking about moving in with his new girlfriend. She was much younger and more enthusiastic about living together than he. He feared she was hoping for what we all eventually discover is impossible—to stabilize a relationship. He was also concerned about giving up his solitude and didn't know how long he wanted the relationship to continue. He asked me if I thought they should live together. "Could this work?" he asked. I was totally ready with "I have no idea" when a voice popped into my head and said, "Of course it can work. As long as you don't expect it to make you happy." So I reported these words to him, and we had one of those smacked on the side of the head moments. We were kind of embarrassed—yes, Buddhists are supposed to know that craving creates suffering—but I guess we still secretly hoped that a relationship would make us happy, if only we could get the circumstances just right.

My new pal and I talked about how relationships can blind us to spiritual teachings quicker than anything. As we said good-bye and I watched him walk away, I wanted to call out, "Don't be afraid to tell yourself the truth about relationships." And then I wondered, What is the truth, exactly? Do I really believe relationships are not supposed to make you happy? When we long for a lasting relationship (as most people I know do), how can we express this longing without also being overrun by fear that we will lose it?

When my husband and I began talking about getting married, we covered lots of topics: who would marry us, whom to invite, what to wear, whether or not we would be able to convince our favorite Cajun band to learn "Hava Nagila." (We were. Shout out to Steve Riley and the Mamou Playboys.)

Then the most important question came up: What would we say to each other to mark this commitment? What were our intentions, and which words expressed them best?

We read various liturgies, Buddhist and otherwise, and talked about what we liked and disliked at other people's weddings. As we read the words countless other couples had spoken to each other, I became increasingly uncomfortable. Most of the ceremonies ended with "I do." I do . . . what? Marriage is a commitment to share love, have sex, and try to stay together with this one person, right?

Marriage may ask these things of us, but I couldn't promise to do them. I knew I couldn't say "I do" to love—feelings change and keep changing. I also knew I couldn't say yes to wanting to have sex with him for the rest of my life—desire is unpredictable. As to asking him to commit to me, which me? I couldn't commit to remaining the same me I would be on our wedding day—I wouldn't. So, if you can't say yes to love, sex, or remaining the one your partner fell in love with—what are you agreeing to when you commit to a relationship?

It's just now, eight years later, that I'm finding out what—apparently—I said yes to.

I said yes to the unfolding, impenetrable arc of uncertainty. I suppose I thought that finding love was an end point, that some kind of search was over and I would find home. My husband and I would leap over the threshold together into whatever we imagined our ideal cottage to be and live happily ever after. But really we stepped through a seriously crazy looking glass. No matter how hard we tried, how madly in love we were, or how skillfully we planned our life together, there was complete uncertainty about what the connection would feel like from day to day. I could give all the love I had (with great joy) and get back a blank stare. I could wake up as my crankiest, most sullen and

narcissistic self, roll over, and greet the face of unconditional acceptance. Or not. It's like the weather: you
can try to read the signs and guess about atmospheric
conditions, but there's no telling for sure. As far as
I can see, this never changes, and the relationship
never, ever stabilizes. So you can't actually guarantee
each other anything. This is how it works. I have no
idea why. But as when I'm listening to a meteorologist
explain why it's going to rain, I think, Who cares? I'm
just trying to figure out what outfit to wear today.

I have discovered that committing to marriage
meant committing to a lifetime of delight and sadness,
inseparable from each other. Every time I look into
my dear one's eyes and feel how deeply we're connected, the moment disappears before I can actually
hold it—and I have to watch it do so. It's excruciating.
It's much easier to do this with your thoughts on a
meditation cushion than with the feeling you get from
his breath on your shoulder as you fall asleep. Now I
get the fact that I will have to accept this as it is, repeatedly, until the end of my life, and that somehow
this is love's road.

I wish I had known that when you live with someone
for a long time, you will experience continuous, mind-
blowing irritation. (Okay, I did know this, but I forgot.) Often the irritation arises when you try to replace
your actual partner with a projection of a partner. He
always figures out a way to tell you how unlike your
ideal he really is, which once you pick yourself up, gives
you yet another opportunity to choose between who

this person is and who you sort of hoped he was. No matter how many times I prompt my husband with the correct lines for his role, he does not get into character. This irritates me. We have to throw away the script and begin to improvise. You're playing you and I'm playing me. Go.

I didn't understand that love does not arise, abide, or dissolve in connection with any particular feeling. It has almost nothing to do with feeling. (Nor does it seem to be making a gesture, committing to stay, becoming best friends, or anything else I might have thought.) Love has become a container in which we live. Through time and riding the mysterious waves of passion, aggression, and ignorance (and boredom), I think we began to live within love itself. At least I did. Each time I opened up, extended myself, accepted what was being offered to me, stepped beyond my comfort zone to embrace him, the structure was reinforced. I no longer have any idea if I love my husband or not. I can't imagine what the feelings I have for him could be called. I've even given up trying to love him. Our relationship is what gives us love, not the other way around.

And of course you're saying "I do" to good-bye. This bond will end. Hello can only mean good-bye, one way or another. Some relationships are just mistakes. People grow and change. Relationships can crater and nobody knows why. If all else fails, certainly at death we will part. Saul Bellow once called this acknowledgment "the black backing on the mirror that allows us to see anything at all," and isn't that just the key to the whole thing? Love and loss are entwined in a way that makes them impossible to separate. The deeper our connection becomes, the more I am aware of the reality of its ending, and the more passionately I'm able to feel my husband's touch. I know this even when I hate him (and he can really be a jerk—I'm not kidding) and when I love him so much that I plead for the opportunity to be married for all our lifetimes.

Each time my love expands by a molecule, it grows a same-size molecule of sorrow. The more I love, the edgier it all feels, and the more courage is required to stay where I am and continue to love. Where one gets this courage, I really don't know. Surprisingly, it just seems to be there. And if you're looking for a crucible in which to heat compassion, this is a really good one. Someone once told me that compassion is the ability to hold love and pain together in the same moment. So at least we're learning something, which is what I tell myself.

Okay, so relationships aren't what you think they're going to be, the feelings are always changing, and you're going to have to say good-bye someday. Why would any-one fall in love in the first place?

In Buddhist thought, the crazy mystery of falling in love, really falling in love, provides ideal circum-stances for giving up your ideas about how things ought to be and instead finding a way to connect with your tenderness and vulnerability over and over. Falling in love offers the opportunity to learn how to give your heart when you know there is no safety and no control over the outcome.

Living with this sense of preciousness and never losing sight of it creates the kind of love that can transform the world. It is based on freedom from prejudice and self-interest. To really love, then, is to give up all expectations and instead rest in your deepest vulnerability.

When the groundlessness of being loosed from your habitual emotional patterns meets the contemplation of impermanence, you suddenly find yourself in very adult territory. Not admitting that a relationship will end cheats the connection of its most powerful dimension. Love remains a bit of bubbly on top of a very deep pond. To maintain the commitment to love while knowing its temporary nature is perhaps the most profound example of fearlessness I can come up with. You will still get incredibly irritated by things such as snoring or dirty dishes, but somehow mixing in these details of everyday life in all its messiness makes loving even more precious. We find ourselves with longings that can never be met, a life made sacred through acknowledgment of death, and a hamper full of stinky socks—and it's all just right.

The source of delight is knowing how to love and begins with being gentle with yourself. With this gentleness, you can touch in with the energy of your fear—whether it is experienced as the heat of passion, the sharpness of anger, or the heaviness of delusion—and convert it to love. In Buddhism this is known as the ability to convert poison into medicine, and there is no situation in which you cannot do this. In fact, I'm told, as you continue to develop a meditative outlook, you actually begin to drop your preference for pleasant events over painful ones because you know that, in any case, it's all going to become medicine with the power to heal. Everything that happens is taken in and worked with as part of the path. There is nothing but value in each interaction, so there is no one in whom you can't take delight.

6

How Not to Be Afraid of Your Own Life: Confidence

EVEN IF YOU ARE able to quell fear of self through gentleness and change discomfort with others into delight, there are still some kinds of fear that are almost impossible to tame. They cause you to hyperventilate, turn your palms to ice, and change your heart into a freight train pounding through the middle of your chest. These are the fears that manifest as intense, non-specific anxiety, panic attacks, and phobias. When in the throes of fears this primal, all you want to do is run away. If it's important to face your fears instead of denying them, how are you supposed to do this with something that defies reason? There is a solution, and it is surprisingly simple.

Captain Denny's Gift

In late 2001, I developed a full-blown case of claustrophobia. Suddenly I was unable to fly, ride elevators, or take the subway without feeling the dizziness, dry mouth, palpitations, and hyperventilation that go with anxiety attacks. I had no experience dealing with fear of this sort and was stunned at how suddenly and strongly it appeared.

The first time I experienced a claustrophobia panic attack I was going to fly from Boston to Denver. I felt a little nervous on the way to the airport, but everyone feels a little nervous on the way to the airport. When I got to the gate, I could feel my heart pounding and my breath becoming shallow. I knew it was going to be very difficult to take my seat on the plane. On the walkway during the boarding process, I felt as if a gallon of adrenaline had been emptied into my stomach. I wanted to push the people in line in front of me to the ground, out of my way.

When I realized I couldn't see the gate back into the terminal, I felt as if I might faint. I pushed my way back out quite rudely and waited until everyone was seated before I tried to board again. I made it to my seat but couldn't bring myself to buckle the seat belt. Sweat was pouring down my back, and I was thoroughly unable to reason with myself. I had flown all over the globe, from Europe to Asia, and once had a job that required trips to London two or three times a month. Who was this new person who could not hang in there?

At the last moment, I grabbed my carry-on bag and slipped off the plane in shame to wait for the next flight and, when that failed, the next one, for which I had attempted to get drunk enough not to care. I drank two double shots of tequila, one right after the other, to numb my fears, but I couldn't get drunk—and I'm not a drinker, so that much alcohol should have done the trick. There was too much adrenaline in my system for the alcohol to take effect. So I called my husband to pick me up, and I went home, utterly defeated, feeling quite sick. Were fear and anxiety going to prevent me from moving about as I pleased?

That night, I booked myself on a morning flight to try again. On this flight I discovered the seeds of a solution to my claustrophobia, although it has taken years to really begin to recover from the problem.

That time, I tried to create the circumstances that would allow me to meditate. I did what I could to keep my breathing slow and steady, and I began to examine my panic attack. I watched it rise up in my chest and turn my limbs to ice. I felt how it seemed to begin in my heart and then move to my lungs and lodge in my throat. I noticed how my own thoughts wouldn't allow the attack to pass; they kept reminding me how trapped I was. I watched the panic rise and fall, ebb and flow, move around in my body, and trigger different thought patterns. In this way, I started to make friends with it, very tentatively, as you would befriend a new neighbor with a pit bull in the backyard. I didn't want to be in this relationship, but here I was and all I could do was grip my armrests for dear life and hope against hope that I wouldn't pass out, that I learned an important lesson about what really calms anxiety.

It began when the flight attendant noticed that I was looking a little, shall we say, maniacal. I guess all that shaking and crying was a dead giveaway. She asked if everything was okay. I told her, "I get a bit claustro-phobic, but I should be fine," and gave her a pleading look. She nodded. Apparently, flight attendants have met many, many claustrophobic people. She brought me a glass of water and asked, "Would you like to speak with the captain?" I said, Sure, why not? I figured that making a relationship with the person in charge couldn't hurt. As she walked away to get him, I real-ized even in my panic that what she really wanted was for the captain to take his own read on my sanity. I guessed she thought there was a chance I could make this a very long flight for everyone.

The captain came out of the cockpit and said, "So, I hear you're a little afraid to fly." I nodded. "Well, don't you worry about a thing," he said. He told me his name was Captain Denny Flanagan and the flight attendant's name was Marie. Between them they had thirty-plus years of flight experience and I was in good hands. "We've got a beautiful day for flying, and I promise I'll get you to Denver safely," he said. I felt like a six-year-old who had just been told by her father that he had frightened the boogeyman off but would sit by the bed all night long, just in case. I relaxed.

Midway through the trip, the flight attendant

walked over to check on me. She handed me a business card and said, "This is from the captain." On the back was a note: "Hope everything is fine. If I can be of further help, don't hesitate to ask. Thanks for your trust and belief in me. Capt. Denny Flanagan." Well, at this point, I never wanted to get off the plane. It seemed like the safest place on earth to be. I slipped Captain Denny's card in my date book, where it remains. I've looked at it countless times on many flights since then, and each time it's helped ward off a panic attack. For me, "Captain Denny" has become a code phrase for "right now, everything is okay."

Kindness Dissolves Anxiety

I developed a personal strategy from this experience. I learned that getting someone to care about me, even for a moment, even if he or she is just pretending, calms me down. When I feel myself getting panicky on a plane or in an elevator, I say to the person next to me, "I get a little claustrophobic. Would you mind talking to me until we take off/you get to your floor?" I've said this to dozens and dozens of people: New Yorkers, Bostonians, Austinites, Los Angelenos, whites, blacks, Hispanics, Asians, priests, punks, old ladies, and teenagers. To a person, *to a person,* every one has turned, looked at me, and said, "I don't mind at all." This question seems to evoke a moment of softening in everyone I've posed it to. Each has made an effort to connect with me, and each time this happens, I calm down. It's like magic. We both open up a little. I've heard all sorts of stories: a singer-songwriter from Nashville told me she was claustrophobic too and gave me one of her CDs; a black preacher kindly read to me from his Bible; a custom home-lighting designer told me about the weird requests he's had from famous clients over the years; a businessman in a twenty-five-hundred-dollar suit told me his wife had the opposite malady—agoraphobia—and that if I wanted, I could hold his arm during takeoff and landing. People respond in the most beautiful ways. Being cared about, even for a moment, is the greatest security there is.

Try this: If you suffer from anxiety, as soon as you notice panic rising, try to reach out to someone. If it seems right, you could simply strike up a little conversation with the person next to you. Or you could reach out to someone you know. Call a friend, write a letter, send an e-mail. Express yourself in some simple way. You don't have to go into the whole story. You can say something like "I'm having a bit of a tough time right now, and thinking about you lifts my spirits. Just wanted to let you know." If you don't want to communicate your fear to anyone, simply make this request within yourself: "Somehow, some way, may this fear build a bridge between myself and others." The key is to counter the energy of fear, which spirals in and down to make you feel heavy and isolated, with the energy of connection, which spirals out and around, lightening the situation on all levels. Make some effort, no matter how tiny, to reverse the spin of isolation that fear brings, by reaching out.

Fear of Death Creates Fear of Life

It's the oldest cliché in the world to say that fear of death prevents joy in living, but it's true. If we really want to talk about how not to be afraid of our own lives, we have to name the six-hundred-pound gorilla. We're all going to die. We have no idea how or when, which for some reason is impossible to remember. We assume we have all the time in the world.

Recently, a dear friend, Clifford Antone, died suddenly. He was a very special and unusual person, the founder of an Austin blues club I worked in. It's not as if he was a saint, but in a sense, he was. On the one hand, he had been to prison twice, convicted of selling marijuana, and not a few joints on the street corner either, more like several tons on a plane from Mexico. But on the other hand, whatever he made, he spent it all, every penny and the entire contents of his heart, on blues music. He opened a nightclub in Austin, Texas, in 1975 and began booking blues greats such as

Muddy Waters, Howlin' Wolf, Albert King, and Freddie King. After the club, he launched a blues record label, then a record store.

Starting in 1985, I worked with Clifford for almost ten years, first as a cocktail waitress, then a bartender, and eventually the manager of his record label. In the mid-nineties, I moved away from Austin, and we didn't see each other much. Shortly before he died, I was in Austin visiting for the first time in several years. Cliff and I had dinner together and spent several hours in sweet reminiscence, recalling crazy things that had happened, such as the time Albert King fired his band in the middle of a set, or when Doug Sahm tried to push me into a swimming pool because I didn't have the money to pay the band.

Almost all the people he idolized were dead. His club still booked blues, but rock acts and comedians brought in the revenue. He was teaching a class at the University of Texas called "The Blues According to Clifford Antone." What he was so passionate about had become academic. His heart was left in the past. The world he loved, had given everything to, and in which he had staked his soul, was gone. I think he felt a bit like a ghost already.

When I heard of his sudden death from a heart attack, I went online to read about Clifford's passing in the local Austin paper. There was a black-and-white photograph of him from the late eighties, in his record store, which housed the record label in the back. I was standing on one side of him, and on the

other was the only other employee of Antone's Record
Label. The two of us were holding our latest albums in
our arms, pretending to show the covers to Cliff, who
was smiling. I was suddenly looking at my own face. I
started to cry. I remembered the exuberance and joy
and wildness of that time, the gifts Clifford had given
us, and I felt so happy and so sad. Working with him
was perhaps the best job I ever had, but also the crazi-
est. I realized that all of it is gone, everything in that
photograph is gone or changed. Record albums are
just about gone. Connie lives in Brooklyn with her
boyfriend and their little baby girl. Clifford is not
here anymore.

As I sit at my desk in Boston writing, I look at the
picture of the three of us stuck on my bulletin board,
surrounded by outlines and notes for this book, a picture of myself at age four, the floor plan of a condo-
minium my husband and I are thinking of buying, and
numerous Tibetan Buddhist symbols and deities. The
spring leaves on the tree outside my window dim the
sunshine that will splash across my desk in winter. Sun
and shade, past and present, happy and sad, here and
gone, this is our life.

Opening to accept the reality of death increases the
capacity to experience life. I'm not convinced that I'm
ever going to stop being afraid of death, my own and,
perhaps especially, others'. I think that might be too
much to ask. But here's what I can do in the meantime: I can tolerate the melancholy of eventual loss for
the sweetness it brings to what is here right now. I can

be patient with myself when I forget that almost nothing matters except how much love I can give and how much love there is in the world. I can have the courage to acknowledge to myself without shame or irony that this is what I really believe. I can rededicate myself each day to the intelligence, grace, and mystery of a truly open heart. My meditation practice has taught me how. I can hold and love my own precious everything, steward it through this crazy maze, and then give it up when it's time to go. I can live my life thoroughly. I can have the confidence to fearlessly engage with everything, even though I know I'm going to die. And I could take a chance on becoming my best, wisest, and deepest self before it's too late. Why not?

What Creates Confidence?

Finding the spark of genuine confidence is surprisingly straightforward. I learned this from my teacher Sakyong Mipham Rinpoche when I went to ask his advice on a project I was producing. It was a small book and CD about different Buddhist meditation styles. The CD featured various renowned teachers guiding the listener through meditation practices from their particular traditions. Each meditation was no more than fifteen minutes long. I wanted to offer these powerful practices in manageable bites, so that anyone who desired could try them out without signing up for a meditation program or reading a three-hundred-page book. But I had learned that teaching meditation is more than just explaining technique; it is a transmission. When a teacher gives meditation instruction, he is also introducing you to his teacher, and his teacher's teacher, and somehow transmitting to you the power of his lineage. Meditation instruction robbed of this power could become a mere self-improvement technique, not a path to awakening. I wanted to be very careful not to screw this up.

Before I accepted the project, I requested a meeting with Rinpoche to ask his opinion. I entered the room and we bowed to each other. He smiled his radiant smile, and we exchanged a few pleasantries. What, I asked him, could make a shrink-wrapped audio recording into a bona fide transmission, into something that would introduce the practice of meditation with the most potency? I hung on his answer. If it was his opinion that this was not possible, that this would be cheating people out of proper instruction, I'd have to consider tabling the project. He thought for a moment and then said this: "The first thing you need to do when presenting a spiritual teaching is to create confidence in the mind of the person studying it."

Of course, I thought. People have to know that this is great so they can relax and trust it. My mind immediately flashed to all the ways I could convey this: bold stickers on the cover with powerful quotes from well-known people, detailed histories of the practices contained, pictures of the teachers in large shrine rooms teaching many people. Then he said, "The way to create confidence is to offer something real." Something real is what you yourself *know* to be true.

You gain confidence, then, from your own authenticity: Your real feelings, thoughts, and ideas; the things you've seen with your own eyes, tested out, and learned from experience. Trusting your own experience is the source of unshakable confidence. The ground of confidence is vulnerability or gentleness, which allows you to open up without fear and to take delight in others without agenda. So now we can begin the cycle all over again: gentleness, delight, and confidence, gentleness, delight, and confidence in an endless loop, a loop that dives deep and carries you far. When you know your mind is as vast as the sky, a few clouds or storms are inconsequential. The sky accepts all forms of weather. It knows that, underneath it all, it's always just sky without end. At this point of understanding, the teachings say, you develop the authentic dignity and elegance that are the hallmarks of confidence. You know how to hold the precious, indestructible jewel of fearlessness no matter what you encounter. There is nothing you can't handle, and so you taste true confidence.

7

Beyond Fear: Joy

DISCIPLINED AND CONSISTENT SPIRITUAL practice changes your experience of everyday life by creating a mysterious sort of congruence between your inner experience and your external circumstances. They begin to align. In other words, when you make a commitment to a spiritual path and honor it as best you can, the road rises up to meet you. After a while, the path seems to be able to deepen on its own. Your experience unfolds with a kind of integrity: the people you encounter, the events that transpire, and the things you do all seem to be part of the same story, one that you weren't quite aware was being told. It's the story of your life and like any good yarn, nothing is put in there without being essential to the outcome. The only thing is, because each person's story is utterly unique, you can't look to anyone to interpret yours and you never quite get to the last page. Now what? After developing all this openness and curiosity, how do you act when you recognize that you can live your life but not control it? In Buddhist thought, you have six options about how to act.

The Six Paramitas

In Buddhist thought, there are six transcendent actions or laws that create a state of happiness. These six—generosity, discipline, patience, exertion, meditation, and wisdom—are called *paramitas* in Sanskrit. They provide pretty infallible guidelines for behavior.

Depending on your religious or cultural upbringing, the concepts of generosity, discipline, patience, exertion, meditation, and wisdom may have positive or negative connotations. You may have been taught that discipline is associated with winning the battle over bad habits, or that wisdom is something one attains after a long course of study. In the context of Buddhism, though, these words refer to very basic capabilities that we all possess. We just need to give ourselves permission to use them.

Each paramita has its own subtleties. It would be a mistake to think that generosity means giving everything away to anybody or that patience is about waiting around and hoping things will change on their own. There is a so-called idiotic version of each of the six paramitas. For example, idiot generosity might be giving everything away to people or situations that are simply going to waste them. Idiot discipline is deciding on a "right" way to do things and never diverging from it. Idiot patience may involve letting yourself get trampled or ignored while you wait for something to happen. Idiot energy is putting all your effort into the wrong thing, and idiot meditation is thinking you get the point when you really don't.

I've noticed that each paramita strengthens the others. None of the paramitas stands alone and when you practice one, the other five are also invoked. When I try to be disciplined without generosity for example, it becomes harsh and strict; exertion without wisdom leads to fruitless behavior, and so on. Keep this in mind as you read about each one.

GENEROSITY

A few years ago, I was visiting a friend in New York City. When I arrived at her apartment, she was sitting at her desk talking with a Tibetan who was staying with her for a few days. He was traveling with a Tibetan lama and acting as his translator. As I walked in, he was telling my friend the story of how his wallet had been stolen by a pickpocket at the bus station earlier that day. He had lost all his money (several hundred dollars) and his airline ticket. "What will you do?" we both shrieked. Being in Manhattan and facing the prospect of negotiating for a replacement plane ticket home with no money while dressed in crimson robes seemed daunting. But he appeared calm. He explained that the sister of a friend was on the way over to lend him a little money. Another friend had offered to guide him through the bureaucratic maze of obtaining a new plane ticket.

Naturally, I wondered if this calm was a front for more turbulent emotions. Anyone would be angry and scared at having been ripped off while in a strange country, especially when he had come to help teach really good things, such as wisdom and compassion. I asked him if he was angry when he discovered his wallet missing. "At first, yes," he said. "I thought about how long that money was supposed to last me, and about my tickets, which are important to me but are now probably lying in a garbage can somewhere. But then I just dedicated it all," he said and smiled.

The Buddhist concept of dedication is one example of what is meant by generosity. Usually we think that we have to secure our own position first and once we have enough (food, money, love) for ourselves, we can give what is left over to others. It's hard to imagine doing otherwise. But I have been taught to view every circumstance as an opportunity to give, and, further, to do so from a genuine sense of caring rather than duty or ethics. (I'm still totally working on it.)

There are three kinds of generosity: ordinary, giving the gift of fearlessness, and giving the gift of wisdom. In a sense, the Tibetan translator gave all three. Although he certainly didn't intend to, he "gave" his money to someone who apparently needed it, and decided after the fact to reframe it as a gift. Instead of wishing he had his wallet back, he relinquished it to the thief. By example, he gave my friend and me the gift of fearlessness. In the midst of difficulty, he relaxed and found a way to soften his heart, without waiting for his problems to be solved first. And he offered the gift of wisdom through his actions. He found a way to be authentically happy without being fatuous or holy. It was done so simply. Understanding the paramita of generosity allowed him to find balance and happiness.

Try this: This very simple exercise can create lovely ripples in the atmosphere around you. The next time you're walking down a busy street, driving on a crowded highway, or sitting in a classroom, look at whomever is around you or passing by and send them this wish: "May you be happy." Take a moment to really take them in. Then wish them well, without any editorializing, such as "May you be happy . . . by wearing clothes that fit you . . . so that you can be less uptight . . ." and so on. You get what I mean. Wish them well and that's it. The important thing is to do this quickly, without thinking about it too much. This exercise trains you in experiencing generosity on the spot, spontaneously and without conditions.

The remaining five paramitas stem from generosity. Generosity is what gives them their soft, workable, transcendent nature.

DISCIPLINE

It would be great if deciding to become generous was enough to make it happen, but as we've all experienced, change rarely takes root based on a good idea. Without discipline, it's all talk. For me, the effort to be disciplined (eat right, exercise, live up to my commitments, and so on) often turns into a feeling of shame that I'm not perfect. But, as I've learned from practicing Buddhism, discipline means something besides holding myself to very high standards and then berating myself if I fail. Actually, discipline comes from gentleness and pliancy as much as it does from focus and precision.

A difficult professional experience taught me the truth of this view. I was meeting with a publisher who had contracted with me to write a book on a topic I was eager to write about. Within weeks we both knew it was a big mistake. They hated what I sent them and I couldn't understand why. We began e-mailing frantically, both of us defending our positions. Neither could see the other's point of view. I took the train from Boston to New York to discuss the problem face-to-face, hoping that a real-time, humane conversation would cut through the anger and misjudgment that can build during faceless e-mail dialogues. To best serve the effort, I spent the evening before the meeting creating a document that outlined our divergent perspectives, listing my point of view in one column and theirs in the other. I hoped that this outline would provide an objective basis for our conversation and diffuse some of the emotion.

Five minutes into the meeting, the publisher took one look at the document I had prepared, stood up, dropped it on the conference room table, turned to me in disbelief, and said, "This is not going to be helpful. Just get me an effing manuscript that I like." He was furious at me. The meeting was over.

I was devastated at this rejection. How could I have missed the boat so completely. I had utterly misjudged the relationship, and I was crushed. I found myself wandering the streets of Manhattan choking back tears, knowing I couldn't write what they wanted and faced with an enormous sense of failure, not to mention loss of income and identity. As I was about to enter a bodega to buy aspirin, I bumped into my dear friend and dharma brother Michael, also in Manhattan on business for the day. Michael, a long-time student of Buddhism, who also happened to be a veteran of New York publishing, would know exactly what I was facing, spiritually and professionally. He took one look at my pathetic expression and asked if he could take me to dinner.

I told him what had happened, how angry I was, how lost, and how destroyed I felt emotionally and creatively. I questioned the strength of my Buddhist practice and acknowledged that I obviously needed to meditate more, a lot more. The fruits of my years of Shamatha had disappeared in an instant. "My practice must be pretty weak if one jerk can completely knock me down," I concluded. Michael looked at me. "So, you think not getting upset is a sign of spiritual progress?" I had hoped that meditation would teach me how to take everything in stride. "Isn't it?" I asked. "No," he said. "It is not. The real sign of progress is how regularly you can come back to rest in the present moment even when it's very uncomfortable." Wait a minute, I thought. I knew how to do this. This was what I had been practicing for all these years: not how to remain sanguine and untouched by emotion but how to *come back* to a balanced place in the present moment. How precisely could I be with my own experience without running away, hating the publisher, or hating myself. The answer is to be found in the paramita of discipline.

Though this lesson came from a highly contentious meeting (the project was published, but we never were able to repair our relationship), it taught me that discipline is the simple ability to come back, to return your mind to the present moment and notice what is happening right in front of you. In meditation, we practice the skill of returning our minds over and over to our breath, with tolerance and kindness. This—the ability to come back—is also the meaning of discipline.

Later on the way home, I tuned into my pain and breathed with it. On the exhalation, I let it all dissolve. With some inhalations I found fury and with others I found sadness, shame, fear, and, eventually, some thoughts about what to have for dinner. It simply began to dissolve on its own. I used the paramita of discipline to come back to the present moment over and over. I stayed with myself until I found the way back to balance and, with balance, the possibility of happiness that wasn't dependent on resolution or revenge.

PATIENCE

I learned about patience from a long-distance relationship. When we fell in love, my future husband and I lived several hundred miles apart. Whenever the subject of living together came up, we became disheartened. He lived in Boston and coparented his son with his ex-wife, and I lived in New York, making a lot of money doing work I loved. And I did not like Boston at all, while I adored living in Manhattan. How to resolve this? Duncan wouldn't consider moving away from his son, and I wouldn't dream of asking him to. Nor could I imagine giving up my own dreams. So for about a year, we saw each other only on weekends. Then it turned into two years, then five. Every few weeks, the subject would come up again and each time we would hit the wall, unable to resolve our dilemma. The pressure kept building. My biological clock had detonated, the financial burden of two households was becoming untenable, and we were both exhausted and cranky from spending so much time traveling. Who was going to give in first? Each time the topic came up, we reiterated our positions, reached our familiar impasse, and felt hopeless. And this is where I learned about patience. Even though the argument was basically the same over and over, we threw ourselves into it wholeheartedly each time. The only reason this was possible was that neither of us took a position by issuing an ultimatum or saying, "Okay, this is it, you have to move here or it's over." Instead, we dove into the conversation again and again. I'm not saying that these years weren't incredibly frustrating, but somehow the net result was to deepen our relationship even though we couldn't resolve our conflict. Instead we watched as our dialogue twisted and turned without censuring or abandoning each other. There was generosity in always remaining open to the dialogue and discipline in the willingness to come back to it over and over. We were patient with each other, even through moments of great impatience. (Well, most of the time.) Eventually my work situation changed. I became self-employed and therefore more flexible. When I moved to Boston, I still wasn't happy about it, but I knew I was going to be with someone who had the patience to stick with me.

"Transcendental patience never expects anything. Not expecting anything, we do not get impatient," says Chögyam Trungpa Rinpoche. When you're patient, you allow things to open and expand at their own pace. Meditation practice had taught me that it is possible to ride the tides of emotion like breath, wave after wave. Eventually, the path to happiness reappears. Without the paramita of patience, one might miss it entirely.

EXERTION

The fourth paramita can be seen as the fuel that animates the previous three. Just as generosity without discipline can become sentimentality, and discipline without patience can become domineering, patience without exertion (energy and effort) dissolves into aimlessness.

When you see the whole picture, you can work within it confidently and you never feel that your energy is being wasted. Whether you're trying to advance in your work, resolve a long-standing fight with your partner, or convince your child that doing homework is good, you will have stamina and feel cheerful. You trust your discernment. You know that what you're doing is intelligently directed, whether or not you see the result right away. You're on the right track, and this sense seems to replenish the energy to exert yourself in all your actions.

No matter how devoted you are to an idea or practice, if you don't try, you won't get anywhere. That may sound obvious, but at the same time I've been astonished at how often I've become excited or interested in something one day and forgotten about it the next. Exertion means you never stop trying.

A meditation practice both requires *and* cultivates

exertion. To get to the cushion definitely requires effort. The practice itself generates energy by enlarging your perspective on whatever may be stressing you out.

When you love something, working at it is a delight, and the more energy you exert, the more you have. I see this dynamic in my own life when I sit down to write in my journal. This has become a treasured part of the day. After a few minutes, something begins to write itself—the solution to a problem, a new idea, an old tale told in a voice I've never heard. Afterward, I invariably rise from my desk with clarity and courage to face the day. I can feel these qualities lacking when I miss a day of writing, and I miss the daily occurrences of synchronicity that seem to flow from this effort. Yet every morning I have to force myself to do this until, once again, the magic of the practice reveals itself to me. The energy for it isn't there at the start. Each time I begin, I think, This is a waste of time. Each time I learn that I was deluded; it is *not* a waste of time. Until that moment, I rely on generosity, discipline, and patience to get me to take my seat so I can rediscover my own vitality.

MEDITATION

As you become more sensitive to the meaning of each of these transcendent actions and begin to make them personal, you can see opportunities to apply them in everyday life. At this point, the paramitas seem to evolve with their own momentum. Long-standing problems begin to come unstuck. The normal, mundane circumstances of your life are revealed as opportunities to develop happiness and maturity. All the while, your heart opens wider and wider, and kindness toward yourself and others increases. If the paramitas were a symphony, the strings, woodwinds, and brass would be in full swing, and the percussion section, those instruments that keep time and emphasize key transitions with a boom or a crash, would be keeping the composition grounded and contained. The fifth action, meditation, is like the percussion section of an orchestra. It gives the performance shape, direction, and a line to follow.

In the context of the paramitas, the word *meditation* is used in a slightly different way than is meant by *Shamatha*. It doesn't refer to the practice of sitting meditation alone. When meditation is viewed as a transcendent action, it refers to the ability to be mindful in all circumstances and to maintain a mind that is stable, undistracted, and able to concentrate. You can remember what the meaning and application of all the other paramitas are and use your focus to put them to good use. You want to be able to use generosity, discipline, patience, and exertion appropriately, correctly, at the right time, as needed. The practice of sitting meditation leads to the paramita of meditation (or mindfulness) by allowing the mind to remain open even under difficult circumstances. With this openness, there is always time to consider the correct course of action. You don't have to respond automatically or habitually.

Keeping attuned to your inner and outer environments can seem like a very complicated job, requiring tremendous effort. In a sense, this is true. But the effort is not to work harder. It's to relax and keep relaxing, to open and continue opening.

Try this: This is my very favorite, on-the-spot technique to recall the calm and wakefulness of the meditative mind. I've used it right before going into a scary, important meeting, in traffic jams, and when I need to fall asleep in a noisy place. It's really simple, and you can do it anytime you want. Bring your attention to whatever sounds are present. As I sit here, I can hear someone washing dishes in the next room, the whir of the air conditioner, and footsteps coming down the hall. Let your ears take in all the sounds. All of them play against a background of silence; otherwise there would be nothing to hear. For example, the pauses between notes in music are just as important to the composition as the notes themselves. Try to tune your ear to the silence. Listen to what is in between or under the sounds you hear, and keep your attention on that. You can always, always hear the silence, even if you're in the stadium during the Super Bowl. Take in the vastness of silence. This exercise is a way to cut into the flow of everyday discursive thought and connect instead with the mind of meditation, which is always equanimous, always attuned to the largest possible reality. From this equanimity, the natural wisdom that is not dependent on intellectualizing can arise.

～　　～　　～

WISDOM

The final paramita is wisdom. Wisdom is knowing how and when to put the first five actions into play based on a clear, profound connection to the truth that exists beyond delusion. When you are using your wisdom, you're no longer fooled by false appearances; you can see through to the heart of your motivations and actions. You can tell real wisdom from conceptualization.

When you have wisdom, you can discriminate properly. You can be soft or precise, come close or move back, take risks or bide your time in the way that is most beneficial to yourself and others. You're neither naïve nor cynical. You can see the humor in just about anything. Your heart is open and also very relaxed.

According to twenty-five hundred years of Buddhist trial and error, the paramitas can be relied upon to lead to happiness and lasting joy. When you can trust them, when you know this to be true based on personal experience, you see that joy actually comes from knowing where joy is to be found.

When you trust your own happiness, you can allow the entire scope of experience to touch your heart. This is the mark of the spiritual warrior. She can hold sweetness, sorrow, rage, and delight equally and fully. She can watch as emotions rise and fall, notice how she reaches out to some and recoils from others, and know that somehow she'll find a way to make whatever she experiences a part of the path. Whether her world is friendly or inhospitable, smooth or rocky, she can abide in it wholeheartedly. A joyful mind is as infinite as the sky and, like the sky, can contain sunshine and storms, snowflakes and hail. Conditions are continually shifting, but the sky is always the sky. It never gives up. From within it, the great sun rises in the east, the moon meets the tide, and the circle is always complete.

8

Freedom from Fear:
A Seven-Day Meditation Program

IT'S EASY TO BECOME convinced of the value of meditation, generosity, patience, and so on. But what happens when, based on theory alone, you try to bring these qualities into everyday life? If you're like me, not much. I need to *practice* these skills over and over before they begin to make sense. The Freedom from Fear program is meant to lead you through the steps that create genuine and lasting change. Now is the time to put a stake in the ground, take action, and see how (or if) these ideas work in your life. You don't have to wait for the perfect day or until you quit smoking or lose ten pounds before you begin practicing meditation to cultivate gentleness, delight, confidence, and joy. The best time is now. Once you make the commitment to try, you'll be surprised to find support coming to you from everywhere you look.

When you set out on the path, the path begins to materialize, but not before.

The Seven-Day Freedom from Fear Meditation Program in this chapter explains how to build meditation and a meditative point of view into your everyday life. It begins with an intensive, solitary thirty-six-hour retreat, and then includes four days back home where you weave Shamatha meditation, journaling exercises, and contemplative activities into your daily life.

I realize that finding the time and space to spend thirty-six hours by yourself is asking a lot. You can try this program without taking a thirty-six-hour break from your daily life, but not starting out this way will weaken the program's transformative power for you. Stepping outside the normal flow of your life offers very important perspective. Please try to find a way to give yourself this gift. You may have to get creative to make it happen, but you can do it. You totally deserve it.

Additionally, the idea of spending thirty-six hours alone may sound a little scary. The skills you've acquired thus far—a meditation practice, Maitri meditation, on-the-spot mindfulness exercises, and, I hope, deeper insight into the way your mind works—can help you through.

Overview

This program invites you to dive right into a meditation practice and experiment with working it into your everyday life through short, periodic practice sessions and daily contemplative exercises. As mentioned, the seven-day program begins with an intensive, thirty-six-hour retreat, during which you will separate yourself from your daily life and immerse yourself in meditation, journaling, and reflective practices. For the remaining four and one half days, you will return to your usual routine, but you will begin and end each day with some of the practices you have done intensely during your solo retreat. The idea is that you will become familiar with these practices and learn how to incorporate them into your everyday life.

Before You Begin

It will be really, incredibly, indescribably helpful if you begin a meditation practice *before* undertaking this program. This way, you'll have familiarized yourself with what it feels like to sit for ten to twenty minutes, how to take the posture in a way that's comfortable, and how to place your attention on your breath. When the seven-day program begins, you'll be able to settle in much more quickly.

I once heard the writer Julia Cameron say, "The first rule of magic is containment," and this is an important concept to bear in mind. Often we think that the way to begin a new program—whether it's a dietary change, a workout routine, or a spiritual practice—is to talk to some friends, read a few books, maybe take a class, and then give it a shot. But there is an additional element that is important to your success: the form you create to stabilize your efforts. Without the proper environment, the excitement and energy of a new endeavor can dissipate rather quickly.

The schedule below is the container for this program. It will create the form and structure that will allow the energy to build. Without this containment, there is no energy or magic. So following the program as carefully as you can is very important.

The Retreat

In order to take a decisive look at your fears and lay the foundation for fearlessness, some distance from everyday life is required. So, the program requires you to spend thirty-six hours, for instance, from 5:00 P.M. on day one until 1:00 P.M. on day three, alone. You'll step out of your life completely and spend one full day and two nights by yourself, with no contact with family, friends, or colleagues. This is very important. Often, our routines define our self-image and dictate what we think about and react to. During this thirty-six-hour period, you'll be thinking about and reacting to yourself—nothing else. You'll take a panoramic view of your own life. You'll give careful thought to what you're frightened of, the effect it has on your life, and who you might be without these fears. You'll immerse yourself in meditation and other contemplative practices. You'll relax with yourself, by yourself, for your-self.

Before you begin, let those closest to you know you'll be engaged in this program for seven days. Ask for their understanding and support. Tell them you may not be able to respond to phone calls or e-mails immediately. As much as possible, prepare things in advance and lean on family, friends, or roommates to handle your usual daily chores. If you are responsible for grocery shopping, stock the pantry in advance. Find people to walk the dog, pick up the dry cleaning, or pay any bills that may come due in your absence. (At the end of the program, you can buy them a present or do something nice for them in return.)

Each day will end by dedicating the intent of your practice to others.

Location

The ideal spot to spend these thirty-six hours would be a spiritual retreat center or health spa—if it's within your budget and geographically convenient. These locations are specifically designed to support a contemplative lifestyle. (See "Meditation Resources" for a list of some centers.) Next best would be staying in a hotel for two nights. It doesn't matter (on the spiritual plane) if it's the Four Seasons or Motel 6. Another option would be house-sitting for two days or borrowing a vacationing friend's house. If you simply can't afford to leave your home for financial or familial reasons, maybe you can find a way to get the house to yourself for thirty-six hours. If none of these are options, not to worry. Perhaps you can commandeer the living room or even make your own room off-limits to others for the intensive period. If you're in a relationship, it won't kill your partner to sleep on the couch for two nights. Your roommates will survive if you decline going out with them for two nights. The idea is to create a safe, nurturing, and solitary space, free from everyday distractions and worries.

If you have no choice but to do this program at home, take special care to stash things that relate to your day-to-day responsibilities. This is not the time to catch up on bill paying or to go over the notes from the last staff meeting. Make sure that all of your favorite distractions are out of reach. This includes your computer, personal digital assistant, the television or radio, magazines, and as you'll see, all books except two.

If you aren't a fan of being alone, the prospect of thirty-six hours with yourself might seem daunting. If you think you need the support of others or just a bit of companionship so you won't go stir-crazy, this program gives you the chance to see if it's true. Facing your fear begins with facing yourself, which along with being scary, exhilarating, and possibly confusing and boring, can also be incredibly grounding. Avoid setting up little escape hatches, such as just one phone call to your boyfriend or a mere thirty minutes in front of the TV. It's important to dedicate yourself to this process wholeheartedly.

Right Space

Creating the right space has nothing to do with setting up the perfect meditation spot or having the best incense. It has more to do with the ambient qualities your intention and discipline impart to your surroundings. Every space has its own feeling-tone, which informs what transpires in that space. If you hear a sad story in a church, it sounds different than it would in a bar or on a submarine. Waking up in a neat and orderly room engenders a different mood than waking up in an unkempt one. Walking through a field at night feels very different than walking through it at noon on a sunny day. Why? The answer is in the space itself. It's a very interesting concept. The space that contains the activity alters the direction of the activity, and vice versa.

Scheduling

Find a time when you can get away for thirty-six hours, beginning at 5:00 P.M. one evening and ending at 1:00 P.M. two days later. If you can do so immediately— great. If it takes six months to find a break in your schedule, that's fine too. Putting it on the calendar actually sets the process in motion. Friday evening to

Sunday lunch may work best, or you might want to wait until a holiday break and do it midweek.

Program

Each of the seven days in the program will include meditation, journaling, and various contemplative exercises. The first thirty-six hours introduce you to each of the practices and are considerably more intense. The remaining four and a half days will follow the same schedule: morning meditation, "free writing," a daily contemplation exercise, and an evening journaling assignment. It's very important to follow the schedule as it is laid out. It's better not to do the program unless you can commit to all seven days. The days are scheduled to build on one another, and if you limit them or spread them out, you will lose momentum. You can expect to go about your daily life but should be able to make time on each of these days for the practices suggested. In other words, choose a week when you expect little outside your regular routine, for example, try for a seven-day period without out-of-town guests or unusually important deadlines.

Food

The program has a dietary component, although not a complicated one: you don't have to give up meat, coffee, or sugar, or eat only organic vegetables, but please simplify the foods you eat during the retreat week and, if you can, for a few days in advance of the retreat start date, so you don't have to spend a lot of time during the retreat figuring out a new food shopping or preparation routine. This will leave you more energy to devote to the contemplative exercises.

For these seven days, the only rule is to eat high-quality foods. This means nothing packaged, processed, or genetically engineered. If you drink coffee, buy organic beans. If you want to eat candy bars, get some good-quality organic chocolate. If you must eat a ham sandwich for lunch every day, make it nitrate-free and on whole grain bread. Instead of sugared cereals for breakfast, try a granola that isn't too sweet. You'll be able to find what you need at a health food store, or do the best you can at your regular grocery store. For beverages, stick with water, milk, and fruit or vegetable juices. Avoid soda unless you'll spend the whole week with a headache if you don't get your diet cola. If you hate to cook and eat only takeout, buy your to-go food from a health-conscious establishment. If you're staying at a hotel where you can't control the food, either bring your own or order the healthiest things on the menu. (If you're fortunate enough to spend this time at a retreat center or health spa, you won't have to worry about the food.) This is not a diet by any means, and you don't have to get overly strict with yourself, but try to cut as many chemicals as you can from what you are eating. Doing so will leave your mind clearer.

Also during this time, please use no alcohol or drugs, because these substances can make meditation very confusing. If you have an alcohol or drug problem or are undergoing medical or psychiatric treatment, please don't start this program. Consult your doctor and wait for a time when you are able to devote your attention to it fully.

If you are taking prescription medications, of course you should continue to take them, according to your doctor's instructions.

If you have any concern whatsoever about this program, please check with a health professional before beginning it.

Supplies

You'll need some supplies for the week. If you want, you can make a "retreat kit." Place these items in a beautiful gift box or purchase attractive wrapping paper to cover a regular cardboard box. The box should be big enough to hold the following:

A blank journal
Pens and/or pencils
A small alarm clock
A self-addressed, stamped envelope (to write a letter
   to yourself)
Two books

In addition to this book (which you'll need as a reference), plan to bring two others. Nothing about how to get over a broken heart or lose ten pounds in ten minutes, and no Harlequin romances or mystery novels. No self-help or guilty-pleasure books. Your books should be about meditation, spirituality, prayer, faith, or any other topic that will teach and inspire you as you make this inward journey. (When I first went on retreat, I took *Zen Mind, Beginner's Mind* by Shunryu Suzuki Roshi, and it was very helpful. I also enjoyed *Turning the Mind into an Ally* by Sakyong Mipham Rinpoche.)

I'm not suggesting these types of books because you need to be deadly serious during the retreat. I suggest them because they will help keep you focused and allow your mind to remain quiet. (See "Recommended Reading" for suggestions.)

SACRED OBJECT

Bring something that you feel represents the highest wisdom imaginable, your best self, or God. It could be a photo or statuette of a deity, a smooth stone from a walk or a vacation on which you felt particularly alive, or a picture of someone you greatly admire. It could be a flower, a shell, or a framed printout of a poem. Make it something of personal significance.

AN OFFERING

Also bring an offering to your own wisdom mind or highest self, as symbolized by your sacred object. There are many things you could choose to offer: the delicate scent of a candle or incense, a bouquet of fresh flowers, a treasured book, or a few river stones. You could offer a small dish of candy. It should be something simple.

WALKING SHOES

ART SUPPLIES (OPTIONAL)

If you like to draw or paint, you might want to bring colored pencils, charcoal, pens, or a small set of watercolors to use as you journal. Keep it simple.

PORTABLE AUDIO PLAYER (OPTIONAL)

If you can make a quiet playlist on your portable audio player and promise to listen to it only, then bring your tunes to listen to on your daily walk.

QUIET PLAYLIST

Taste in music is very personal, so what I find relaxing and beautiful, you might find boring. Whether you like Sinatra or Madonna, Bach or Wu-Tang Chan, choose slow-tempo, spare tunes.
Here's what works for me.

Ammeh Kimia . . . . *Jamshied Sharifi*
Bach Unaccompanied Cello Suite No. 1 in G major,
    BWV 1007. . . . . *Yo-Yo Ma*
Blue Gardenia . . . . *Dinah Washington*

Body and Soul . . . . *Mel Tormé*

Change Is Gonna Come . . . . *Sam Cooke*

Copperline . . . . *James Taylor*

Funny How Time Slips Away. . . . . *Willie Nelson*

In a Landscape . . . . *William Orbit*

Indigo Burrell . . . . *Ronnie Earl*

In the Evening (When the Sun Goes Down) . . . . *Ella Fitzgerald*

Kothbiro . . . . *Ayub Ogada*

Live to Tell . . . . *Madonna*

Mary . . . . *Patty Griffin*

Moonlight in Vermont . . . . *Johnny Hartman*

My Funny Valentine . . . . *Chet Baker*

My One and Only Love . . . . . . *John Coltrane and Johnny Hartman*

On the Other Hand. . . . . *Randy Travis*

'Round Midnight . . . . *Mel Tormé*

Satta Massagana . . . . *The Abyssinians*

Someone to Watch over Me. . . . . *Frank Sinatra*

Tabula Rasa . . . . *Arvo Pärt* (various performers)

The Way You Look Tonight . . . . *Tony Bennett*

Trouble Man   . . . . *Marvin Gaye*

Wichita Lineman . . . . *Glen Campbell*

You Are Too Beautiful . . . . . . *John Coltrane and Johnny Hartman*

You Changed My Life . . . . *Charles Brown*

You Don't Know What Love Is . . . . *Dinah Washington*

YOGA MAT (OPTIONAL)

If you have a yoga practice, by all means, bring a mat.
But no DVDs. Remember, you won't be watching TV

at all. If you want to do yoga, do the poses you know and are comfortable performing. Re-create the sequence of the poses from memory or as feels best to you.

MEDITATION CUSHION (OPTIONAL)

If you have a meditation cushion, you could bring that. If not, you can use a chair, sofa cushions, or even the bed as your meditation spot.

Don't overthink your selections. Go with your gut, and you'll find you have what you need when you need it. Keep this simple and relaxed.

When you have chosen a start date, gathered your supplies, and figured out how to meet your dietary needs, you're ready to begin.

THE PROGRAM

Day One: The Day of Slowing Down

*Quiet minds cannot be perplexed or frightened but go on
in fortune or misfortune at their own private pace,
like a clock during a thunderstorm.*

—ROBERT LOUIS STEVENSON

All spiritual practice begins with slowing down, letting the concerns of everyday life drop away, and turning one's attention inward. This evening, allow your body to slow down. If you're not at home, don't rush through unpacking. When you sit down to journal or meditate, take your seat gently. Don't multitask. Do one thing at a time. Breathe deeply. Allow your mind to expand. Know that, for the next thirty-six hours, you're going to let it rest quietly. When body and mind slow down, the spirit comes forward.

As you begin the program, realize that learning these practices could mark a turning point in your life, so really go for it. "Leap, and the net will appear," as the saying goes. You can trust that when you take your first step, even if it appears to be into thin air, the net begins readying itself to catch you. The leap and the net come into existence at the same time.

So as you do this inner work, the world around you seems magically to create the circumstances and coincidences that will support you best.

5:00—6:00 P.M. SET UP

Whether you're in your bedroom, a friend's house, a hotel, or a retreat center, do what you can to make sure your space will be available by 5:00 P.M. There is nothing magical about 5:00 P.M., but it's helpful to have a clearly delineated start time and to begin your retreat with a sense of discipline. If you're using your bedroom, make sure that you've cleaned up and put away distracting or irritating things. Make sure you have the groceries you'll need for the entire thirty-six hours. If you're going to a friend's house, take care to have checked out and prepared the space beforehand. Come a little early to do so, but be ready by 6:00 P.M.

If you're at a hotel, ask that your room be in a quiet spot. Unplug the telephone. Turn off your cell phone and stash it. Cover the TV with a blanket, or swivel it around to face a wall. When you shut the door, your space should feel good—safe, but maybe a little exciting.

Unpack your retreat box. Create a shrine by placing the object that represents your highest wisdom somewhere neat and clean. A bookshelf, bedside table, or windowsill is good. Since this object represents what is most precious to you, you don't want to place it on the floor, in a closet, or amid a bunch of cookie crumbs. Next, place your offering next to or in front of your item. Do so with a sense of gratitude for this gift of solitude and quiet.

Choose a place for your meditation. It could be facing your shrine or not. If you have a cushion, set it up in a clean and, if possible, out-of-the-way spot. If this isn't possible, it's no big deal. Simply decide where you're going to sit and be prepared to set your cushion there during meditation periods. If you aren't using a traditional cushion, decide whether you'll be sitting on a chair, a sofa, or the bed. If you've chosen a chair or sofa, make sure it's one you can sit up straight in, back unsupported, feet on the floor. If you're going to sit on the bed, figure out a way to stack pillows so that you can sit comfortably but upright. You could sit cross-legged or on the edge of the bed or with your feet on the floor. If your feet don't reach the floor, stack some pillows or cushions under them to bring your knees level with or slightly above your hips.

Unpack your clothes, toiletries, groceries, and so on.

6:00—7:00 P.M. JOURNALING, DINNER, CLEANUP, WALK

Open your journal. For your first journaling exercise, take about twenty minutes (or longer if you wish) to make note of what your senses are able to take in. For now, leave your feelings behind, forget about whatever motivated you to do this program, and look around you. What are your surroundings like? What type of furniture does this room contain? What are you sitting or lying on, and how does it feel? Is it comfortable? What colors can you see? What can you smell or hear? How does it feel to be in this room—not how do *you* feel, but how does *the room* feel—is it serene, jumbled, warm, plain? Does it feel like a happy, unhappy, or neutral place to be?

Note how your body feels. Scan from your feet to your head, and jot down whatever you notice. "The bottoms of my feet hurt. My back is so comfortable against these pillows. My chest feels warm. My eyeglasses are pinching the bridge of my nose a tiny bit." And so on. This is a way of attuning to your environment and settling into it by making contact with its energy through the placement of your attention. When you're finished, set your journal aside and get ready for dinner.

Dinner should either be prepared already or easy to prepare. Whether you cooked in advance, picked up takeout, or need to cook now, keep it simple and nourishing. It shouldn't take more than thirty minutes to prepare, nor should it be a bag of cookies or chips. Eat something you know is basically good for you. As you eat, you can read one of the books you brought, or do nothing but taste your food.

Clean up.

Take a twenty-minute walk unless it's freezing cold or you're in a dangerous neighborhood. Walk around the block. Take your time. This walk isn't meant to be athletic. Walking is an uncomplicated way to connect with your body and digest your food. If you're on familiar turf and you have a portable audio player, you can listen to your quiet playlist while you walk. Otherwise, pay attention to your breath and take in your surroundings.

7:00—10:00 P.M. JOURNALING, RELAXATION, SLEEP

Get your journal out again and make yourself comfortable. During this exercise, you'll be turning your attention inward to begin a dialogue with yourself. The following sentences are like little prayers, requesting the blessings of whomever or whatever you believe to be the source of blessings. If you have no such beliefs, this is fine. If it's more comfortable to you, don't think of them as prayers but look at them as markers that set your intentions in motion, little ways of telling yourself the truth about what's on your mind. What you write should be fairly simple and straightforward. Don't rush, but don't spend an inordinate amount of time finding the perfect words either. Write what comes to mind. You can always tweak this later.

Please help me to _____ so that I may_____.
Please guide me to _____ so that I may _____.
Please show me _____ so that I may _____.
Please teach me _____ so that I may _____.

Here are some examples of things you might say:

Please help me to quit smoking so that I may be
    healthy.

Please guide me to the people or circumstances who
can help me find a job doing work I really love so
that I may express myself fully.

Please show me how to talk with my sister so that I
may stop fighting with her.

Please teach me how to have confidence so that I may
ask for what I'm worth.

Keep it simple, but if you're inspired to elaborate,
feel free. You can use a sentence a page, explaining
each item. Whether or not you elaborate, be sure to
fill in the blanks.

Now, dedicate your prayers or wishes so that they
may serve others too. If it's helpful, go back to page 63
and reread the explanation of the dedication of merit.
Spend a few moments composing your wish that whatever benefit may have accrued through these exercises
also be put to work for the benefit of others. It can be
as simple as "I hope that what I learn can serve others," "I don't know how, but may my work here be
helpful to others," or "I dedicate whatever good has
arisen today to a higher power."

You could use the following traditional verses as a
dedication of merit if you like:

By this merit may all attain omniscience.

May it defeat the enemy, wrongdoing.

From the stormy waves of birth, old age, sickness,
and death,

From the ocean of samsara, may I free all beings.

The important thing is that your generosity be genuine. Touch in with the natural tenderness you experienced during Maitri meditation, and let your words emanate from that feeling.

Now read either of the books you've brought or relax until bedtime.

Try to get to sleep by 10:00 or 11:00.

Day Two: The Day of Self-Remembering

But when the self speaks to the self, who is speaking?—the entombed soul, the spirit driven in, in, in to the central catacomb; the self that took the veil and left the world.

—VIRGINIA WOOLF

In the rush of everyday life, in trying to meet the demands of family, work, and health, we simply forget who we are. While returning phone calls, reading e-mail, doing errands, taking care of others, *trying* to take care of self—we don't have time to remember who we are. Our energy is continually going out, directed at people and tasks. Today, you turn that energy around and direct it to yourself. With great respect, appreciation, and dignity, turn inward. Let today be the quietest day of your life.

7:00—7:30 A.M.

Wake up. Fix your coffee or tea.

7:30—8:00 A.M. SHAMATHA MEDITATION: 20 MINUTES

Go to your meditation spot. Take your small alarm clock and this book, if you want to review the meditation instructions before practicing. I've included a refresher on Shamatha practice here. If you have brought a candle or incense, light it. Take a few moments to settle in and find the correct posture. When you feel that you're ready, set your alarm clock for twenty minutes and begin to practice. When the alarm sounds, turn it off and sit for a few moments before you rise.

Dedicate the merit.

SHAMATHA INSTRUCTIONS

Find a quiet, comfortable place to sit. If you are planning to sit on a cushion on the floor, dress in comfortable, loose-fitting clothing.

Minimize distractions.

Take your seat and review the points of posture: Sit on an even surface, legs crossed comfortably or feet flat on the floor (if on a chair); back is straight but relaxed, hands are resting on the thighs, palms down, eyes are open but soft, gaze is forward and down to a spot a few feet in front of you, mouth is closed but lips are slightly parted.

Before beginning the actual practice, remind yourself what you are doing, that you are about to meditate, that you will give it your all, and that during this brief time everything else can wait.

Now you are ready to start.

∽   ∽   ∽

8:00—8:30 A.M. FREE WRITING

If you look into your mind, you will see it's like thousands of butterflies whirling about! You can hardly trace a single idea in this complexity.
A way to bring clarity to the mind is to write down your immediate thoughts and feelings in response to the events of the day, and then ponder them.
If you emphasize one particular problem in this writing,
it will gradually lead to all others.

—J. KRISHNAMURTI

You'll need your pen and journal for the exercise. Sit comfortably on a chair, the sofa, or your bed. This journaling exercise is called free writing, automatic writing, or as named by Julia Cameron in her book *The Artist's Way*, "morning pages." You will write three pages—whatever comes to mind, write it down. Simply keep your hand moving across the page, and don't worry about making your words elegant, grammatical, or sensible. There is no need to be logical. Just keep going. If you can't think of anything to write, just write "I can't think of anything to write" for three pages. Free writing has a number of purposes: It clears the head of gobbledygook, lets you know what mood you're in right now, offers solutions to problems, gives space for whining and complaining, and connects you directly to your most creative impulses. Writing three pages should take about thirty minutes. No one will ever read these pages. You don't ever have to read them either.

Free writing is a powerful tool—it teaches you how to listen within yourself and trust what arises. Our minds are usually speedy and busy. This exercise slows your thinking down, thought by thought. As you continue to tune in, you will be able to hear all your different voices: encouraging, shaming, wise, childish, brave, and insecure. There are dozens of voices, making dozens of yous, including a you that grew up believing what your teachers or parents said, a you that urges you forward, protects you from pain, believes you are lovable, or jeers at you from the sidelines. Through attention, they begin to separate out. Through your writing, you can learn how they speak (like a child, a stern aunt, or your best girlfriend) and what brings them forward in your inner dialogue. In free writing, you can begin to hear the voices "talk" to one another, engaging in long-standing feuds (the part who believes you're lovable versus the part who jeers at you), creating escape routes (your risk taker versus the one who keeps you safe), and figuring out how to love (codependent you versus warrior goddess you).

As you get to know yourself, you will find—

invariably, there are no exceptions—wisdom you had no idea you possessed. It comes forward when you least expect it to point you in the right direction, tell you whether or not to stay in school or take a job, help figure out if falling in love with so-and-so is a brilliant move or a confused one, teach you to distinguish what brings healing from what reinforces neurosis. Sometimes your writing will be one whine after another or endless to-do lists. But if you make three pages of writing a daily practice, and if your inner wisdom knows you will keep the appointment, it will show up for you. The only rule is to begin the practice *without agenda*. Simply sit down, pick up your journal, and start writing. Writing longhand engages this process more than writing at the computer. It is more intimate and relaxed, and it forces you to slow down.

It takes practice to hear your best self, and you certainly can't force it to happen, but if you are patient and respectful, your inner wisdom will come out. It wants to come out when the ground has been prepared properly, and somehow, disciplined practice is that proper preparation. Claudio Naranjo, a pioneer of the Human Potential Movement, once said, "Only repetition invites spontaneous variation." This is a wonderful description of the fruits of discipline. It's only by playing the same piece over and over again that the musician learns to improvise skillfully.

Here are a few recent examples from my freewriting journal that illustrate how the practice begins. If I can embarrass myself this way, so can you.

4-25-06

As usual, I'm kind of late getting to what is most important. I feel a little speedy—maybe in part because yesterday was such a buzz. In deep conversation with PR. Very motivating conversation with Michael. Had a short interview. A lot of talking, which made me tired. When I click on conversation with PR, I feel full and safe for some reason. Odd because the conversation was about shadowy things. But it makes me feel connected up somehow. I should make note of that idea I had after I hung up the phone yesterday. I have an endless list of boring things to do today. . . .

4-26-06

It's very, very cold where I'm sitting right now, on a platform waiting for the train to NYC. A very chilly April morning and I feel very nervous. Am looking forward to going shopping this afternoon. I want to look good. Have to consider how to answer Lisa's questions. I can talk about it in simple, everyday terms without being fake, superficial, or egg-heady. Tomorrow I have to co-teach that course. It's the first class. When will I have time to do the reading I'm supposed to do? I can get to it after lunch, should have a little break. I have to figure out a better way to treat the things that are most important. Shouldn't just shoehorn them. It would be great to slow down, or to even know how. . . .

4-27-06

Oh it is so lovely to wake up in the morning and start the day in complete quiet. It just feels so good and safe to me. So enjoyable and relaxed and there are so many possibilities. Here's my flash on their response to the articles I wrote. I think they think it's decent. But do I think it's substantial enough? Getting ready for breakfast with Rob, I hope his kids are okay. It was so fun to work with him on those music projects and I want to remember to lend him that book. Oh no I hope I'm not getting a headache, I really, really want to have a lot of energy today. . . .

I'm sure you get the idea. My writing almost always starts out in this vein. But in the ten years I've been doing this exercise, it usually (not always) happens that somewhere within these three pages, I tell myself something important—a cool idea, a smart solution, or unspoken feelings. This happens probably 80 percent of the time. In the other 20 percent, I have run the gamut from making endless to-do lists to suddenly encountering an enormous reservoir of rage, grief, or disappointment. I've also heard the voice of someone who is unbelievably petty and that of someone who is shockingly profound. You never know.

8:30—10:30 A.M. BREAKFAST, CLEANUP, RELAXATION

I mean really relax. If you do yoga, unfurl your mat and do some stretches or, even better, restorative poses. Read for pleasure. Go back to sleep. Let yourself slow down.

10:30—11:30 A.M. JOURNALING EXERCISE: PART 1

Questions are a way of focusing attention. Focusing attention in the present moment is a way of connecting with genuine wisdom. Think about each question until you sense its personal meaning for you, and then begin writing. You can make your answers as short as a sentence or as long as you like. After you're done, set the answers aside. We'll come back to them at the end of the program.

1. What three things do I love about myself?
2. What three things scare me about myself?
3. How can I honor my body? How do I honor my body?
4. What can't I say?
5. What can't I feel?
6. What do I want written on my tombstone?
7. Who do I need to forgive?
8. Who needs to forgive me?
9. What is unfolding in my life right now?
10. Who are my true friends?

11:30 A.M.—12:00 P.M. SHAMATHA MEDITATION: 20 MINUTES
Dedicate the merit.

12:00—3:00 P.M. LUNCH, CLEANUP, RELAXATION

3:00—3:30 P.M. SHORT WALK

3:30—4:00 P.M. SHAMATHA MEDITATION: 20 MINUTES
Dedicate the merit.

4:00–5:00 P.M. JOURNALING EXERCISE: PART 2

11. What is unmourned in my life?
12. What really ignites me, if I let it?
13. How do I manipulate others?
14. What are my addictions?
15. Who have I been listening to that I shouldn't?
16. Who haven't I been listening to that I should?
17. What aspirations am I not allowing myself to manifest?
18. What fears are ruling my life and how I make decisions? About love? Sex? Money?
19. What am I doing to preserve comfort? Get approval? Earn love?
20. What is difficult for me to receive? Offer?
21. What can't I admit about myself?

5:00–7:00 P.M. DINNER, CLEANUP, RELAXATION

7:00–7:30 P.M. SHORT WALK

7:30–8:00 P.M. SHAMATHA MEDITATION: 20 MINUTES

Dedicate the merit.

8:00–10:00 P.M. READ, RELAXATION

Asleep by 10:00 or 11:00 P.M.

Day Three: The Day of Intention

A good intention clothes itself with sudden power.

—RALPH WALDO EMERSON

Today marks a transition. As you go through the activities of the morning, let the solo part of your retreat go. Don't try to hold on to it or run away from it too quickly. Use the writing exercises to remind yourself of your motivations, wishes, and aspirations in bringing meditation practice home.

The final meditation session before you go home (or back to your everyday schedule) includes Maitri or loving-kindness meditation. This is to help make sure to include others in your efforts.

7:00—7:30 A.M. WAKE UP. FIX YOUR
COFFEE OR TEA.

7:30—8:15 A.M. SHAMATHA MEDITATION:
30 MINUTES

Dedicate the merit.

Note that this session is a little bit longer.

8:15—9:00 A.M. FREE WRITING.
USE THIS PROMPT: WHAT I NEED TO TELL
MYSELF TODAY IS . . .

Just for today, use this prompt to get yourself started writing. Write whatever pops into your mind. For some reason, it's helpful to write quickly, perhaps because doing so helps to bypass your inner critic. Don't worry if you make a few false starts when writing with a prompt. Just keep trying. (This free writing session is a bit longer to provide time for experimentation.)

9:00—10:00 A.M. BREAKFAST, CLEANUP

10:00—11:00 A.M. SHAMATHA AND MAITRI MEDITATION

This morning, make Maitri (loving-kindness) meditation your practice. Begin and end with ten minutes of Shamatha. After you've sat for about ten minutes, start your Maitri practice. I've included a refresher on Maitri practice here. When your Maitri meditation is over, resume Shamatha for ten minutes or as long as you like.

Dedicate the merit.

MAITRI INSTRUCTIONS

Remember, in this practice you touch your own natural tenderness and begin extending it out in wider and wider circles, first to yourself, then to a loved one, then to a friend, then to a stranger, to an enemy, and finally to all beings. This practice can be done seated in formal meditation posture, sitting in an easy chair, or lying in bed. Eyes can be open or closed.

Begin with yourself. See yourself in your mind's eye and think for a moment about how hard you work to create happiness for yourself and others, make a living, express yourself, accomplish something in this life. You make so much effort. Sometimes it works and sometimes it doesn't, but somehow you keep trying. With these thoughts in mind, allow yourself to wish for your own happiness. Say to yourself, silently:

> May I be happy.
> May I be healthy.
> May I be peaceful.
> May I live with ease.

These phrases are used in traditional Maitri meditation practice. If these words don't feel quite right to you, you can substitute others.

Let your awareness of yourself and your efforts to be happy fade. Bring someone you love to mind, someone who, when you think of him, causes your heart to soften. It could be a parent, partner, child, or dear friend. If you can't think of anyone who makes you feel this way, bring to mind a pet or a character in a book or movie who has moved you. Think about how hard this person has tried to create happiness, how he has struggled and worked. Then send this loved one the loving-kindness phrases:

May you be happy.
May you be healthy.
May you be peaceful.
May you live with ease.

Next, bring to mind a friend. It doesn't have to be your best friend, although it could be. This should be a person who has been kind or helpful to you or let you lean on her. Think about her efforts to be happy and send the phrases to her.

After this, call a stranger's face to mind and wish him well too. It's totally possible to wish someone well when you don't know him.

Now think of an enemy—someone who has wronged you. Let your enemy's face come to mind. Know that this person too is just trying to be happy, no matter how strange her attempts may look to you. Send her the phrases, and try to really mean it.

In the last stage of the practice, let any particular person go. Realize that all the people in the world have friends and enemies, people they love, and those they are indifferent to. Each of these people, every single one, is trying to find happiness. All creatures are. Take a few minutes and wish that all beings could be happy.

Dedicate the merit.

Let the practice go, and relax for a few moments before getting up.

11:00—11:30 A.M. SHORT WALK

11:30 A.M.—1:00 P.M. A LETTER
TO YOURSELF

Get out your journal or a piece of paper and write a letter to yourself. In your letter, describe how you're feeling and what you may have learned about yourself or noticed about your life during this retreat. Review any feelings, discoveries, delights, and irritations that have come up during this time of solitude. Go over the lists of questions you answered and circle the five most important questions, the ones you don't want to forget. Make note of any ideas or emotions you'd like to explore further. You could voice your wishes about your life, remind yourself of all the things you're doing that you're proud of, or express yourself about anyone or anything you like. You could encourage yourself to be strong and brave in whatever areas you think you need such encouragement. The letter could be one sentence or twenty pages long.

Now turn to the requests you created during the first journaling exercise (see page 163). Do they strike you any differently? Would you like to change the wording of any of your answers? Add additional requests? Once you feel satisfied with your sentences, tear this page out of your journal or write all the sentences on a new piece of paper. Put your request with the letter you wrote to yourself in a self-addressed, stamped envelope, find a mailbox, and send it to yourself before you return to your regular life.

At this point, your solitary retreat is over. I salute you! It takes a lot of planning, not to mention courage, to pull something like this off. It's daunting to devote yourself to a period of intensive introspection. I'm so glad you were willing to take this chance. Congratulations!

As you pack up to leave (or transition your space back to its original purpose), go slowly. If you begin to feel emotionally unsteady, know that this is very natural. (But if not, it doesn't mean you've missed the impact of the retreat!) Being in a protected, quiet space can provide relief from the hassles and problems you face in daily life. Going back to your normal routine can feel like a loss. Retreat participants may also feel sad because they think they'll never be able to reestablish this contemplative atmosphere in their everyday lives.

If you're feeling sad or worried, there are a few things you can do. Most important, remind yourself that you can trust this process and the practices you've learned. They've been around for thousands of years, and millions of people have had their lives transformed by them. If you stick with it, meditation will transform yours. And be gentle with yourself. Try not to zoom back to normal speed right away. If possible, give yourself the opportunity to ramp up to your normal responsibilities slowly. Most important, when you get home (or restore your home to its normal state), sit down on a chair, your bed, or your meditation cushion and meditate. It doesn't matter if you practice for five minutes or thirty minutes, making the effort immediately to establish your meditation practice at home base is a powerful gesture. So don't unpack, don't check messages, and don't start making grocery lists. Sit in Shamatha meditation for a few minutes first, and then resume your ordinary routine as you like.

15 MINUTES BEFORE BED AT HOME: JOURNALING

Recap how it was to make the transition back home.
　Shamatha Meditation: 20 minutes
　Dedicate the merit.

Day Four: The Day of Change

I am always doing that which I cannot do, in order that I may learn how to do it.

—PABLO PICASSO

The first day after your solo retreat is for focusing on bringing what you've learned home and beginning to integrate meditation and contemplation into your daily life. Take it slow. Don't be discouraged if you don't feel transformed or if bringing meditation into your life is more difficult than you thought it would be. Remember who you are and what prompted you to begin this program. Remember what you discovered on your solo retreat and how important those discoveries are to you.

7:00–7:30 A.M. (OR TWEAK IF NEEDED FOR YOUR SCHEDULE) SHAMATHA MEDITATION: 20 MINUTES

Dedicate the merit.

7:30–8:15 A.M. FREE WRITING

TODAY: CONTEMPLATE A PRECEPT

In Buddhism, the Five Precepts represent the five first commitments you make to the spiritual path. These are vows not to kill, steal, lie, engage in inappropriate sexual conduct, or use various intoxicants. Without adhering to the precepts, it's said, it is pretty much impossible to progress along the path. I'm not suggesting you *commit* to the precepts, only examine their presence in your life.

The precepts sound pretty straightforward, but when you start to focus on them, they become a bit more complicated. Take lying, for example. You may think of yourself as a fairly truthful person. I do. Nonetheless, when I started paying attention, I found that I was lying all the time. I would refer to something that happened "last year," when it really happened five years ago. Or I would tell my husband, "I'll be right home," when I *knew* I was going to spend another hour at the office but I thought telling him would upset him and I didn't want to get into it. These untruths aren't the worst things in the world, but they create a kind of gray film on everyday interactions. Most of the time, I tell these little lies because I'm too lazy to think for the extra second about how to be precise or how to respect others by telling them the truth despite what I think their reaction might be. But these types of lies are sneaky. When you start paying attention to how you may obscure the truth, you can begin to hold yourself to a higher standard of mindfulness and greater effort.

The precept "Don't kill" has its own set of complications. I'm sure you're not running around stabbing people or taking aim at pigeons, but if you bring your attention to this precept throughout the day, you might find small infringements. Every spring, ants mount an initiative to occupy the bottom floor of our house, and every spring I fight with myself about killing them. This kind of killing counts as a trespass against the precept, but at some point I allow myself to get careless about stepping over or around the ants because I'm just so sick of having them in the house. You may eat at a restaurant that serves shellfish which was probably still alive right before it was on your plate.

Of course, we destroy things all the time in ways we have no idea about—we step on bugs we haven't seen, our cars emit fumes that kill trees or birds. We can't possibly watch out for all these precepts violations. But focusing your awareness on the way life and death are continually cycling in and out of very mundane circumstances brings a heightened sense of the preciousness of life. Stopping to think about extending respect to all living creatures can make us more respectful of our own lives as well.

The other precepts operate with similar subtlety: When you borrow some file folders from a colleague without telling her, is that stealing? If you continue to find excuses to hang around your best friend's husband because you think he's cute, is that inappropriate sexual conduct? And while you may not drink or take drugs, what are you doing when you eat a cupcake or turn on the television to distract yourself from something upsetting?

So pick a precept and begin paying attention to how you follow it or break it throughout the day. You don't have to adhere to the precept or make any changes in your life. In fact, it's better if you don't, because if you are trying to change, your mind won't be open to taking in your actual experience.

6:00—6:30 P.M. SHAMATHA MEDITATION: 20 MINUTES

Dedicate the merit.

BEFORE BED: JOURNALING

Journal about the precept you chose. What and where did you notice its themes today? Did you notice it affecting your thoughts or actions? If you had taken the precept formally, would you have broken it today? Where?

Day Five: The Day of Heart Opening

My religion is very simple. My religion is kindness.

—DALAI LAMA

When the body slows down and the mind turns inward, the heart naturally and gracefully expands. Tenderness and care for others become a joy for the self. Today is devoted to touching in with this truth.

6:50–7:30 A.M. SHAMATHA MEDITATION: 30 MINUTES

Dedicate the merit.

Start a little earlier and increase your practice by ten minutes.

7:30–8:15 A.M. FREE WRITING

TODAY: CONTEMPLATE A PARAMITA

Contemplate one of the paramitas, the six actions that support fearlessness. Refer to Chapter 7 to refresh your memory of the meaning of generosity, discipline, patience, exertion, meditation, and wisdom. As you did with the precepts, choose one, say generosity, and notice where it appears or is lacking as you move through your day. If you chose generosity, notice who arouses your generosity easily, and with whom it becomes difficult. Notice the generous or ungenerous gestures of friends, colleagues, even strangers or people on TV.

6:00—6:30 P.M. MAITRI MEDITATION

For this evening's meditation, practice Maitri (loving-kindness). Begin and end with two or three minutes of Shamatha.

Remember, in Maitri meditation you get in touch with your own natural tenderness and begin extending it out in wider and wider circles, first to yourself, then to a loved one, then to a friend, then to a stranger, to an enemy, and finally, to all beings.

BEFORE BED: JOURNALING

Journal about the paramita you chose. What were your observations about how it appeared (or didn't) in your day?

Day Six: The Day of Friendship

A friend may well be reckoned the masterpiece of nature.

—RALPH WALDO EMERSON

Today your focus is going to be on appreciation for those who have shown you kindness. Remember the journaling exercise you did back on Day Two? One of the questions was "Who are my true friends?" You may have listed a dozen names, or none, or maybe just that of your pet. It doesn't matter. Today you're going to consider the topic of friendship.

Kalyanamitra is a Sanskrit word meaning "spiritual friend." A spiritual friend is someone who offers you a chance to deepen your spirituality. A spiritual friend can come in the form of a very generous and encouraging person who has taught you a lot. But it can also be a person who has caused you pain and forced you to grow spiritually. For example, I consider the boyfriend who broke my heart to be a spiritual friend. I certainly didn't feel that way at the time, but now I know that this experience gave me a glimpse into the illusory nature of emotional suffering. So, if you benefited from someone by learning something, seeing things more clearly, or becoming more devoted to loving-kindness, then this person was a kalyanamitra.

6:50—7:30 A.M. SHAMATHA MEDITATION: 30 MINUTES

Dedicate the merit.

7:30—8:15 A.M. FREE WRITING

Make a list of the people from whom you have learned the most. It may have been through a good experience or a difficult one, in the past or in the present. Choose one or two people, and bring their faces to mind. You are going to write each of them a letter of gratitude, but before doing so, pause to give thought to the nature of their kindness. Let yourself feel what it was like to have received what they brought to you. Tell them what you learned, how you learned it, and how it helped you. Explain to them the impact this has had on your life. Offer your appreciation to them. You can choose to mail your letters, or not.

Go about your day as usual.

6:30—7:00 P.M. SHAMATHA OR MAITRI MEDITATION

Dedicate the merit.

Day Seven: The Day of Commitment

If you do not change direction, you may end up where you are heading.

—LAO TZU

6:50—7:30 A.M. SHAMATHA MEDITATION: 30 MINUTES

Dedicate the merit.

7:30—8:30 A.M. FREE WRITING AND JOURNALING

In addition to free writing, take some time to journal about what has occurred in the last seven days. What were your expectations before you began? How have they been confirmed or altered? Think back to your thirty-six hours of solitude. What was that experience like? What has it been like to meditate every day? Has it been difficult to make the time? Easy? How has it felt to consciously bring spirituality to your everyday life? What have you learned about yourself or those who are important to you? What are your intentions regarding your spiritual practice going forward?

Go about your day as usual.

6:00—6:30 P.M. SHAMATHA OR
MAITRI MEDITATION

Dedicate the merit.

6:30—7:00 P.M. OFFERING OF
GRATITUDE

To close your seven-day program, take a few moments to make an offering of gratitude. You could offer gratitude to those who made it possible for you to do this program; to your family or friends who supported you emotionally or by taking some of your responsibilities off your hands. You could give thanks by writing them a note, giving them a gift, or simply thinking good thoughts of them and wishing them well.

You could offer gratitude to yourself for putting in this effort. A program such as this demands a lot of focus. You may have confronted difficult and painful feelings; you may have taught yourself how to let go, enjoy stillness. It takes courage to embark on a journey such as this. Thank yourself for making this happen.

You could offer gratitude to the wisdom that animates all existence: God, Self, Being. Give thanks for the seen and unseen support that surrounds you.

Finally, dedicate the merit of this entire week to the greatest good. Know that, as you return to your everyday life, you are doing so from a position of increased strength and vulnerability. Go slow.

AFTERWORD

THE PROCESS OF WRITING this book has given me ample opportunity to work with my own fears. I've spent many hours dancing around with self-doubt and the possibility of rejection. Writing it has meant moving from my seat in the back of the meditation hall to the "teacher's cushion" up front, and doing so has felt quite uncomfortable. Am I being a show-off? Do I really know anything? How dare I presume to speak on these topics? Finding my daring required me to shift my vantage point considerably, and therefore my expectations about my own voice and what it would say. I began the process with the sense of embarking on a noble challenge. I would only find out if I could do this work after it was finished.

At first, the words flowed out onto the page. I've spent more than a decade ruminating on the wisdom of Buddhism (the "Buddha-dharma") and witnessing it mix with and change my life, so I knew there was a lot of material to work with. I felt that trying to write on this topic was making good use of my practice. Although I certainly hoped that the book would be good for you, the reader, I knew it would be great for me; I would have the opportunity to metabolize what I've been taught and then crystallize it into words for others' benefit. This seemed like the best possible thing I could do with my life.

As I always do when working on a project, I came to my office every day, sat in front of the computer, and waited to see what would come out. I wrote piece after piece, the way one who is making a quilt creates patches. Because I don't work well with outlines, I trusted that when I was ready to lay them out together, the pieces would connect easily through a wisdom greater than my own. This was what had always happened before.

It didn't happen this time. The first attempt to sequence the pieces of writing left me feeling like Shelley Duvall in *The Shining* when she looks at Jack Nicholson's book and sees that it consists of "All work and no play make Jack a dull boy" typed out thousands of times.

I felt what I had written was a bunch of gibberish. The months of work seemed wasted, and I felt foolish to have presumed to write on this topic. How could I possibly sound more vacuous and poseur-like? I was such a loser. I ran out of my office and drove home, sobbing and shaking. I felt that I had failed myself, my publisher, and my teachers. I began compiling lists of people I could call for advice, frantically scanned successful books for their secret formulas, and finally, collapsed on the couch with *Seinfeld* reruns. (Not that there's anything wrong with that.)

The next morning, I awoke feeling numb and heavy. I drove to my office in anguish, gut clenched and hands gripping the steering wheel. How would I ever make this mess into something coherent, and how would I meet my deadline? I unlocked the door and looked at the past week's collection of dog-eared books, scribbled Post-it notes, and unwashed teacups. I wanted to run away. I thought to myself, How can I possibly get back to work? I am so shaking with fear right now. Then I remembered that the book was called *How Not to Be Afraid of Your Own Life,* and I knew what to do. Nothing.

I sat down to practice meditation in the area of my office designated for this. I lit a candle, took my seat, and offered a traditional opening chant, which contains a line that goes "Grant your blessing so that confusion may dawn as wisdom." I longed for this so much. I felt the power of the lineage, of all those who had chanted these lines before me, in these words and in my tears. I felt myself begin to relax. I remembered the instruction to stop fighting fear and instead begin to observe it, feel into it, take its pulse. I remembered that exploring fear with the agenda of feeling better would not work. I tried for a few minutes anyway, but then I just sat with my fear. I connected with its energy, and it felt sickening. I felt my throat begin to close and could hear my heartbeat through my chest. I watched as my mind filled up with dreadful, detailed thoughts about how inadequate I was. I stayed with the bad feelings. The fear was just below the surface of my skin, quivering, hot and cold at the same time. I noticed how I tried to struggle away from the fear. I tried to stop the escape attempt and simply rest with the fact that I was struggling. I saw my desperate hope that my meditation would release me from fear. I tried to drop that agenda. I saw hope well up with anticipation of release and sink down when release evaporated. And on it went, and on and on.

I sat with myself in this way for about an hour. Many times I thought, Okay, that's it, I feel better now, back to work. But I waited a little bit longer, and the fear uncoiled like a snake at the base of my spine and moved up and down, up and down, until the energy of fear seemed to fill the room. Although I still felt tremendously uncomfortable, I also noticed a kind of growing warmth. I was paying attention to myself. I was sitting with myself as I would hold a still sleeping child twisting from a nightmare. I wasn't angry with her, and there was no sense in trying to talk her out of it. All I could do was hold her gently until she was awake enough to know where she was. The Zen teacher and poet John Tarrant says, "Attention is the most basic form of love; through it we bless and are blessed," and that seemed really true. I rediscovered the part of myself that knew how to come back to balance, and I began to connect with her more and more. I remembered my unshakable faith in the Buddha-dharma, and with that, a sense of basic trust returned. I wish I could say that I leapt from the cushion fully centered and peacefully in control. I didn't. But I felt blessed anyway, and tremendously heartened. Fear had left me.

As I stated at the beginning, everything contained in this book is based on my own experience. The topics and exercises are those from which I've benefited most. In the end, there is nothing else to write about, nothing but what I can personally attest to.

If there's anything at all you might take away from this book, it's the notion of personal responsibility and the encouragement to view your own experience as the noble path. You can trust yourself and that life has meaning and is leading you somewhere. You can discover who you are beyond fear and, in so doing, discover the unique meaning of your own experience.

When we're afraid, we search for means to control the uncontrollable. When we find a system of thought that promises security, we want to believe in it wholeheartedly. It would be easy to subsume our own mind in a particular dogma and then call that faith. But lasting, genuine faith can arise only from experience. It can't be a gesture of the intellect or the emotions, only an organic arising. Turning your attention inward then is actually the best way to reach God, however you define that presence. What you find will not look like what others find. By fully owning your own mind and inhabiting your own body, you begin to know the truth. Meditation is the ground, path, and fruition of this activity.

APPENDIX:
FREQUENTLY ASKED
QUESTIONS

Why should I meditate?

Meditation introduces you to the way your mind really works so that it supports your intentions and aspirations instead of thwarting them. Meditation also gives your mental processes a rest, so that when you need them, they're strong and fresh.

How often should I meditate?

It's best to try to meditate a little bit every day. Frequency is much more important than duration. Ten minutes a day every day is preferable to an hour every Sunday. If you don't have ten minutes, try to take a few moments on the bus on the way to work or before falling asleep to tune in to your breath and let your mind relax. If you're stuck in traffic, it's not a good idea to meditate, but you can turn off the radio, shut off your cell phone, slow down, and let yourself enjoy the quiet.

What happens if I skip a day?

It's okay. Don't make yourself feel so guilty that you never want to practice again. Just return to it the next day.

Is meditation hard to learn?

Meditation is not hard to learn. It takes about fifteen minutes to learn the technique. It's actually a return to your natural mind state, not the acquisition of a new one, so you already know how to meditate, you just may not know that you know.

Do you have to sit on the floor?

If you can sit comfortably on a cushion on the floor, great. If not, it's perfectly fine to sit in a chair. You will get the same benefits. Just be sure to follow the same posture instructions.

What if I can't stop myself from thinking when I'm meditating?

There's no problem. It's impossible to stop thinking; this is what the mind does. It's very important to realize that meditation is not about clearing the mind of all activity. It's about coming into a different, gentler, more playful relationship with your thoughts.

I'm busy from morning till night. How can I possibly make time for this practice?

Try several very short periods—five minutes or so—of meditation a day. You could do this at your desk, on the bus, or anyplace you can sit quietly. You can connect with the mind of meditation for a minute, or even for a few seconds. (Whenever you think of it, let your attention rest on your breath.)

I have strong religious beliefs that have nothing to do with meditation. Will I have to give any of these up?

No. Meditation is nontheistic. It doesn't require you to believe in any doctrine.

Meditation can get so boring. Am I stuck? Doing something wrong?

The meditation master Chögyam Trungpa Rinpoche has said boredom is actually a sign that things are going well—you are slowing down. Resistance to the form is dissolving. Your mind is settling.

How do I know if I'm doing it right?

If you're continuing to practice and are remembering to return your attention to the breath, everything is going fine.

People report all kinds of amazing experiences and insights, but I never have anything like this. Am I doing something wrong or missing something?

No. Everyone's experience of meditation is different. It is completely individual. In any case, the instruction for amazing experiences is the same as the instruction for thoughts: Gently let them go and return to the breath.

What am I trying to accomplish?

Absolutely nothing. Meditating with a goal or in order to accomplish something is not giving the practice a fair shake. Instead, let yourself off the hook, step off the self-improvement treadmill, and simply be with yourself in your natural state. The practice isn't about achieving something. It's about letting go.

What if my leg falls asleep or I have an itch? Can I move?

Yes, but move mindfully. When you notice the urge to move, wait a moment. Notice what this urge feels like instead of responding to it automatically. Then rearrange to make yourself comfortable.

I'm really loving this and want to share it with everyone in my family. Can I teach them how to meditate?

It's preferable to direct them to a meditation center for instruction from an experienced teacher. See "Meditation Resources" for possibilities.

RECOMMENDED READING

Pema Chödrön. *The Places That Scare You: A Guide to Fearlessness in Difficult Times.* Boston: Shambhala Publications, 2001.

Dalai Lama, and Howard C. Cutler. *The Art of Happiness: A Handbook for Living.* New York: Riverhead Books, 1998.

Sakyong Mipham Rinpoche. *Ruling Your World: Ancient Strategies for Modern Life.* New York: Morgan Road Books, 2005.

Sakyong Mipham Rinpoche. *Turning the Mind into an Ally.* New York: Riverhead Books, 2003.

Shunyru Suzuki Roshi. *Zen Mind, Beginner's Mind.* Boston: Shambhala Publications, 1970.

Chögyam Trungpa Rinpoche. *Cutting Through Spiritual Materialism.* Boston: Shambhala Publications, 1973.

Chögyam Trungpa Rinpoche. *Shambhala: The Sacred Path of the Warrior.* Boulder, Colo.: Shambhala Publications, 1984.

MEDITATION RESOURCES

If you find that you'd like to make meditation an on-going part of your life, please seek instruction from an authorized teacher. This is important. Even though the technique is very simple, the impact it may have is not. Without guidance, it is extremely easy to lose focus.

Shambhala Centers

The meditation practice in this book is called *Shamatha* (peaceful abiding), as it is taught in the Shambhala Buddhist lineage, of which I am a part. It was brought to the West by the Tibetan teacher Chögyam Trungpa Rinpoche and is now directed by his son and spiritual heir, Sakyong Mipham Rinpoche.

To find a Shambhala center in your town, please visit www.shambhala.org.

Retreat Centers

These centers offer in-depth programs:

Dai Bosatsu Zendo
Livingston Manor, N.Y.
www.daibosatsu.org

Esalen
Big Sur, Calif.
www.esalen.org

Green Gulch Farm
Muir Beach, Calif.
www.sfzc.org/ggfindex

Insight Meditation Society
Barre, Mass.
www.dharma.org/ims

Karmê Chöling
Barnet, Vt.
www.karmecholing.org

Kripalu Center for Yoga & Health
Lenox, Mass.
www.kripalu.org

Omega Institute
Rhinebeck, N.Y.
www.eomega.org

Shambhala Mountain Center
Red Feather Lakes, Colo.
www.shambhalamountain.org

Spirit Rock Meditation Center
Woodacre, Calif.
www.spiritrock.org

Tassajara Zen Mountain Center
Carmel Valley, Calif.
www.sfzc.org/tassajara

Meditation Supplies (Cushions, Bells, Candles)

Samadhi Cushions and Samadhi Store
1-800-331-7751
www.samadhicushions.com

Ziji
1-800-565-8470
www.ziji.com

ACKNOWLEDGMENTS

WRITING THIS BOOK PROVIDED this beginning student with the precious opportunity to work full time on understanding the Buddha-dharma, and for that I am extremely appreciative. The first person I want to thank is Lisa Senz at St. Martin's Press. Without her vision, stewardship, and energy, this book would not exist. She improves everything she works on, and for that I am grateful, as I am to my editor, Sheila Curry Oakes, for her patience and precision, which made this a much better book than the one I originally delivered. Thank you to Susan M. S. Brown for such intelligent and careful copyediting. And to all at St. Martin's Press who have been so interested and enthusiastic, not to mention incredibly fun to be around: Matthew Shear, Sally Richardson, John Sargent, John Murphy, Dori Weintraub, John Karle, Tom Mercer, Bob Podrasky, and all the sales, marketing, production, and promotion folks: thank you, thank you, thank you.

In addition to my teacher Sakyong Mipham Rinpoche, I offer gratitude for the blessings received from the wisdom of Chögyam Trungpa Rinpoche, Tulku Thondup Rinpoche, Pema Chödron, Traleg Kyabgon Rinpoche, Reginald Ray, Dzigar Kongtrul Rinpoche, and Chokyi Nyima Rinpoche.

A deep bow to my *kalyanamitras* for their spiritual friendship and for sharing their understanding with so much generosity: Adam Albright, Josh Baran, Hazel Bercholz, Richard Borofsky, Emily Bower, Maya Breuer, Michael Carroll, Stephen Cope, Richard and Danna Faulds, Michael Greenleaf, Daniel Hessey, Konda Mason, Michael Potts, and Patricia Reinstein—and especially to Sam for his intense generosity.

I'm grateful to the following friends and colleagues for reading this manuscript at various stages and/or offering their comments, insight, and support: Sari Boren, Emily Bower, Maya Breuer, Sandy Kaye, Melanie Lowe, Melvin McLeod, Cindy Matchett, Richard Pine, Patricia Reinstein, Lindsay Sproul, Eden Steinberg, and Paul Zakrzewski helped me shape the direction of this book and find my voice.

Special thanks to my publicist and sister, Beth Grossman, who definitely knows how to make things happen. Her tireless encouragement and greatness of spirit never cease to amaze and inspire.

I wrote portions of this material at Karmê Chöling, a

Buddhist retreat center in Barnet, Vermont. A writer could not ask for a better place to work. Thank you to Bill Breuer and Ella Reznikova.

To my family, including my stepson, Duncan Browne IV; my loving parents, Julius and Louise Piver; my siblings, David Piver, Zea Piver, and Carol Hanna; and to my adored husband, Duncan Browne III, without whom the center would not hold, I love you.

DEDICATION OF MERIT

By this merit may all attain omniscience.
May it defeat the enemy, wrongdoing.
From the stormy waves of birth, old age, sickness, and death,
From the ocean of samsara, may I free all beings.

By the confidence of the golden sun of the Great East,
May the lotus garden of the Rigden's wisdom bloom.
May the dark ignorance of sentient beings be dispelled.
May all beings enjoy profound brilliant glory.

ABOUT THE AUTHOR

Susan Piver is the *New York Times* bestselling author of *The Hard Questions,* a series of books designed to provoke self-inquiry. She is the founder of Padma Media, a company that works with spiritual teachers and health experts to create at-home programs. She has worked with Baron Baptiste, Mark Hyman, Brooke Siler, Andrew Weil, Rodney Yee, and others.

She has practiced Buddhism in the Shambhala Buddhism lineage since 1995. In 2004 she graduated from Buddhist seminary, and in 2005 she became an authorized meditation instructor. She leads retreats and workshops internationally and contributes articles on Buddhism, meditation, and relationships to a variety of publications. For more information, visit www.susanpiver.com.

Susan Piver lives in Boston, Massachusetts.